# Pick a Number

# Pick a Number

## *The U.S. and International Accounting*

Second Edition

Roger Hussey
Audra Ong

*Pick a Number: The U.S. and International Accounting*



First published in 2018 by
Business Expert Press, LLC
222 East 46th Street, New York, NY 10017
www.businessexpertpress.com

ISBN-13: 978-1-94709-893-0 (paperback)
ISBN-13: 978-1-94709-894-7 (e-book)

Business Expert Press Financial Accounting and Auditing Collection

Collection ISSN: 2151-2795 (print)
Collection ISSN: 2151-2817 (electronic)

Cover and interior design by S4Carlisle Publishing Services
Private Ltd., Chennai, India

First edition: 2014

10 9 8 7 6 5 4 3 2

Printed in the United States of America.

# Abstract

For many years, individual countries decided their own rules and regulations for company financial accounting and reporting. As the world became more global, problems began to arise. A company could make a profit for the year if the rules in its own country were applied, but this could turn into a loss if another country's rules were used. This did not make sense.

Investors were hesitant to buy shares in foreign companies, trading businesses were careful when the financial stability of foreign suppliers and customers could not be established, and companies wanting to list on a foreign stock exchange, for example, New York, experienced difficulties.

To prevent this confusing and misleading state of affairs, attempts were made at the international level to agree on what the rules, known as accounting standards, should be for financial accounting and reporting. Those standards are now issued by the International Accounting Standards Board (IASB). From 2002, the standard setter in the United States, the Financial Accounting Standards Board (FASB), was actively engaged with the IASB in attempting to converge U.S. regulations with international accounting standards. Although several successes were achieved, the "convergence project" faltered and faded away in 2014.

These events are important not only to accountants, but to everyone who has been dealing with a company. This could be investors, employees, customers, banks, suppliers, and the tax authorities. If you are interested in the financial performance and status of a company, you need to understand the accounting rules, their changes, and the reasons they pursue an international set of standards.

This book describes in nontechnical language:

- The process for setting accounting regulations in the United States
- Attempts to establish international standards and the barriers confronted
- U.S. involvement in international activities through a process known as convergence
- Successes and failures in agreeing on international rules
- Differences that have halted convergence and the U.S. strategy
- The possible developments in U.S. and international corporate reporting

The U.S. direct involvement in international standard setting brought about many changes in the calculation of the numbers shown on a company's financial statements. This book focuses on the main changes and how and why they happened. It highlights frauds and questionable activities and describes the FASB's efforts to ensure that financial statements do not mislead their users. We also discuss the differences that led to the United States withdrawing from international standard setting and the future of corporate reporting both in the United States and internationally.

One technical issue that the reader needs to bear in mind is the international terminology. The early accounting standards were issued by the International Accounting Standards Committee (IASC) which was founded in 1973. This body issued International Accounting Standards (IASs). In 2001 the IASB took over from the IASC and retained the IASs that it had issued. However, the IASB decided that any new standards it issued would be named International Financial Reporting Standards (IFRSs). We are now in the position that we have IASs and IFRSs addressing different accounting issues and both sets of standards are enforceable. Where it is of no importance whether a standard is an IAS or an IFRS we have used the generic term "international standard."

## Keywords

accounting standards, conceptual frameworks, convergence, Financial Accounting Standards Board, fraud, International Accounting Standards Board, Norwalk Agreement, principles-based approach, rules-based approach

# Contents

# Preface

Two accountants applied for the same job. The final interviews were with the chief executive officer (CEO). He asked the first candidate "What is three plus three?" The immediate answer was "six." The same question was asked to the second candidate who looked the CEO in the eye and said, "What do you want the answer to be?" The second candidate got the job.

The message of this story is that the answer in accounting can depend on the rules and regulations that are used. Unfortunately, those rules are subject to change. Even more confusing is that some countries have different accounting rules. This means that the amount of profit or loss made by a company may depend on whether U.S. rules, UK rules, or those from another country are being used. If those rules are altered, the figure of profit may change too.

*Pick a Number: The U.S. and International Accounting* examines and explains the problems—legal, technical, and political—that influence the calculation of the numbers that appear on a company's financial statements. The outcomes could vary—the numbers may assist you to make decisions, confuse you, or even obscure fraud and misleading practices. Put the decision on what number to pick at the international level and chaos could occur.

Chapter 1 sets the scene by explaining the need for regulations, the basic accounting concepts underpinning these regulations, and the procedures in the U.S. Board (Financial Accounting Standards Board, FASB) and the Securities and Exchange Commission (SEC).

Chapter 2 describes the problems of individual countries setting their own accounting regulations and the background to the proposals, some 40 years ago, to develop international accounting standards that every country would follow.

The increasing U.S. involvement in the discussions and its decision to converge its accounting regulations with international ones are described in Chapter 3. Chapter 4 explores the problems and issues that resulted in the United States not proceeding to the full convergence of its regulations with those of the International Accounting Standards Board.

Chapters 5 reviews the position of the United States and considers possible future developments. This includes both changes in technology and the growth in companies disclosing nonfinancial information.

# Acknowledgments

All books come to fruition because of the help of several people. First on our list are the students and professors at the University of Windsor who commented on several sections of the book. Our thanks are also due to our research assistant, Ashley Laramie, who helped guide the book through its final stages. Finally, our gratitude is given to Rene Caroline Balan and her team for seeing the manuscript through the editing stages to final publication.

# CHAPTER 1

# The Development of National Accounting

## About This Chapter

Many people assume that accounting regulations affect only the work of accountants. They believe that accounting is a complex, mysterious subject that is best ignored. This is not the case. The methods and assumptions that are used to measure the financial performance of an organization affect many people.

Managers may find that profit has declined, not because there have been any changes in the organization, but because of the way that accountants measure their activities. Consequently, managers may have to change the way they work to achieve their expected profit. Potential and existing investors and other creditors track the financial performance of companies. Even if you do not make a direct investment, you may be in a pension scheme or other organization that places its funds on the stock market. If performance changes for the worse, they may decide to reduce their involvement with that company. Employees and customers form their own opinions of the reputation of a company. That reputation is also, to a large extent, tied strongly to financial performance.

Accounting rules and regulations form the magnifying glass we use to examine corporate performance and the performance of directors and managers. In this chapter, we discuss the reason for accounting regulations and how they have developed in the United States. We explain the structure and authority of the powerful Securities and Exchange Commission (SEC), which has no equal in any country. We also look at the work of the Financial Accounting Standards Board (FASB) and the financial information available about the organizations you invest in, work for, and shop with.

## The Need for Regulations

Companies are major forces in our society. They provide employment, manufacture goods, offer services, and, if successful, generate financial returns for investors. Many of the financial transactions undertaken by companies and the economic events that affect them can be measured in different ways. If you are a manager, a shareholder, a lender, or any individual or institution with dealings with a particular company, you need to know the reliability of the financial information that is available. You also require financial information that is relevant to the decisions you are making.

Unless there is some form of guidance, accountants may adopt different approaches to record the same type of transactions. The following examples show some of the dilemmas that can arise:

1. You are a retail company and purchase goods from a supplier during the year. Needless to say, the prices of goods have risen slightly in some months. At the end of the year, you have some unsold inventory. Do you value the inventory at the price you first paid for the goods at the beginning of the year, the price paid at the end of the year, or an average for the entire year? How you value your closing inventory will affect the amount you calculate as your profit for the year.
2. A customer, who is well known to you, has received goods from you at the end of the year and promised to pay you at the start of the New Year. Do you count this as a sale of goods in the current year or only when you receive payment?
3. Another customer has selected the goods he requires and has asked you to keep them for collection. He expects to collect them in two months' time when payment will be made. Have these goods been sold? Should you record any profit you have made?
4. You purchased some land for $250,000 about 10 years ago and you consider it is now worth $350,000. What amount do you put in your accounting records? Does your decision depend on whether you intend to sell the land or to keep it?
5. You own a machine that cost $200,000 five years ago. You believe that it will last another five years, but it is technologically outdated

and needs replacement. If you sold the machine you would only obtain $30,000 for it. What value should you put on the machine in your accounting records?

6. You sell heating systems for factories complete with a five-year maintenance contract. You have just installed a system for $180,000 with a five-year contract for $40,000. What should you record as the sales figure in the current financial year?

Problems such as these confront accountants every day. Often, there are alternative solutions and they can all be argued to be "right." The solution chosen, however, often has an impact on the profit figure and what the financial strength of the business appears to be to outsiders.

It is essential that accountants agree on the solution that is the most appropriate so that the recipients of corporate financial information can understand the picture presented. The users need to be assured that an inappropriate solution has not been selected for the purpose of putting the financial affairs of the business in a better light.

To prevent users of financial information from being misled, accounting is conducted according to regulations. That regulatory framework, known as Generally Accepted Accounting Principles (GAAP), consists of legislation, stock exchange regulations for public companies, and accounting standards.

## Generally Accepted Accounting Principles

GAAP consists of a set of regulations with substantial authoritative support. GAAP is the framework that regulates companies in their recording of economic transactions and events to produce financial statements such as the income statement, balance sheet, and statement of cash flows.

In the United States, the FASB for many years issued Statements of Financial Accounting Standards (SFASs). Later in this chapter, we explain how the FASB Accounting Standards Codification (ASC) is now the official source of guidance in the United States. Many countries use International Standards and in Chapter 2 we explain the development of both International Accounting Standards and International Financial Reporting Standards (IFRSs).

Although, in all countries, legislation and stock exchange requirements are important in determining the type of information companies should disclose, by far, the most dominant and pervasive influence on accounting practices and the specific nature of financial disclosures is accounting standards.

Standards determine how a company's profit is calculated and its apparent financial strength. To understand the scope of these standards, we need to appreciate the main players that comprise the standard setting side of the regulatory framework. We also need to understand the concepts and assumptions they apply in deciding the regulations.

## Accounting Concepts and Assumptions

At this stage, we are going to consider some basic assumptions used by accountants, most of which are contained in the accounting literature. We will return to some of the assumptions in later chapters to demonstrate how they are applied to the financial statements in practice.

### *Business Entity Concept*

This assumption means that the accountant is preparing financial statements only for the activities of the business and not for the personal financial activities of the owners. The financial statements will inform us about the financial performance and position of the business, but very little about the financial situation of the owners. We will be able to obtain information about transactions between the owners and the business, such as when the owners invest money into the organization, but we will not have information about the activities of the owners that do not relate to the business's operations. For this reason, it is helpful to think of a business as an *entity* that is completely separate from its owners when you are preparing financial statements.

Unfortunately, the complexity of modern business relationships has made it more difficult to define the entity for reporting purposes. It is no longer possible to think of a physical entity such as a factory or a shop.

Companies enter into agreements and relationships that they consider to be mutually beneficial. The problem is identifying which corporate body is responsible for what, and who should therefore report the financial outcomes of business activities.

### *The Consistency Concept*

This concept has two aspects to it. The first is that there must be a consistency of treatment by an organization for transactions and events of a similar nature. An accountant cannot treat a transaction in a particular way and then later change to another method for a similar transaction. For example, if you decide to write off company cars over five years you cannot later change this to 10 years, unless there is a valid reason for doing so.

Second, an accountant must apply the same accounting treatment from one accounting period to another unless there is a very good reason to change. If a company has a policy of deciding that funds spent on certain items are considered long-term assets, it cannot then choose to treat the funds as day-to-day expenses. The purpose of the consistency concept is to reassure the users of financial statements that accountants do not change their accounting methods to show a more favorable picture of the organization.

Consistency is critical to ensure the comparability of the financial information of an organization over a series of time periods. Of course, there may be a very good reason for a company to decide in one financial period to change its accounting policy. Accounting regulations set out the circumstances in which companies can change their accounting policies and the information that should be disclosed in such situations.

### *The Matching Concept*

If we want to know the performance of an entity for a financial period we need to account for the expenses it has incurred in that period and match them with the revenue it has generated. By doing this, we calculate the profit or loss of the company for the financial period. The timing of revenues and expenses is therefore critical in calculating the profit for the period. But remember that these transactions may not involve the immediate movement of cash. They are usually credit transactions. As users of financial information we want to know the profit made on transactions, irrespective of cash movements, but we also need to know the flows of cash.

Revenue tends to be time based and can be identified with a particular financial period, unless it is a long-term contract spanning several periods. Expenses may not always be contained within a specific time period and therefore a degree of judgment may be required to match the expenses with the revenue.

### *The Money Measurement Concept*

This concept assumes that only the items that are capable of being measured reliably in financial terms are included in the financial records. Reliability in measurement is normally a requirement to recognize (i.e., enter into the financial records) an economic transaction or event.

This assumption should not cause any problems. If a company buys 20 tons of steel at $500 per ton, then $10,000 worth of steel inventory is entered into the financial records. If a company has 100 employees and pays them each $300 per week, the weekly wage bill is $30,000. What the company is unable to do is to enter into its records how much those employees are *worth*. They may be highly skilled and the company may not be able to operate without them, but a money measurement cannot be calculated reliably to account for this asset.

Another example is the case in which a successful business has built up a good *reputation*. It is known for making excellent products, keeping to delivery times, and offering an excellent after-sales service. You will not usually find a money measurement for these attributes. However, there are regulations that allow what is known as intangible assets to appear in financial accounts.

Increasingly, entities have found that their most important assets for generating future benefits are not physical assets, such as buildings and machinery, but assets that have no physical substance. Examples are computer software, customer lists, patented technology, and trademarks. A detailed knowledge of the regulations is required to establish which intangible assets can appear in the financial statements and how they should be valued.

### *Historical Cost Concept*

The principle of this concept is that the amounts shown for assets are based on their original cost, which is when the transaction or event took place. No adjustments are made for subsequent changes in price or value. The concept has the great merit of being extremely reliable. If you wanted to know how much a company had paid for an item of equipment, you would only need to look at the actual payment.

This method also has some great disadvantages. A company might have purchased some land in 1970 for $750,000. It might decide in 2016 to buy an additional piece of land that is identical in all ways to the original purchase but the price is now $1,000,000. How is the user expected to interpret this information in 2016? In the financial statements, the amounts originally paid for the land will be added together and the company will disclose that it has an asset of $1,750,000. The question the user most likely wants to be answered is "What is the current value of the two pieces of land?"

It may be for some reason that the present value of the land has decreased. The land bought for $750,000 in 1970 may be valued at only $500,000 in 2016. It could be that there has been environmental degradation, the local economic market has collapsed, or adjacent buildings or roadwork have impacted the value. Whatever the reason, accountants need to decide the basis for the amount they put in their financial statements.

There have been some attempts to replace historical cost accounting with a different method that better reflects current values. There are several methods, each with its own advantages and disadvantages. These methods make the information more relevant to the decisions being made by the user, but the reliability of the information may be uncertain. Once the regulations allow companies to depart from the rigors of historical accounting, there is always the concern that users will not understand the figures, or that the company will exploit the regulations to present misleading information.

## Manipulating the Figures

The purpose of accounting regulations is to ensure that accountants adopt identical and acceptable methods for similar transactions. This enables users of the financial statements to follow the progress of a company over a period of time or to compare its financial position with other companies, confident in the knowledge that all are applying the same methods of accounting. The sophisticated regulations and governance structures and processes in the United States do, as far as possible, achieve that end.

However, excluding financial fraud, there are still issues that may weaken the reliability of financial statements. We have given some examples of accounting dilemmas where the treatment of a particular economic event or transaction could be viewed in several ways. It is practically impossible to establish regulations so comprehensive that every eventuality is addressed and to ensure that the regulations are scrupulously followed. The danger is that loopholes will be found to mislead users on the financial status of the company.

For example, closing inventory valuations and revenue recognition offer opportunities for the unethical company to manipulate their profit figures. Fraudulent practices can be found in all countries and are used by both large and small organizations. A small business may wish to reduce its profit to lower the tax it has to pay and the large organization may wish to inflate its profit to increase its share price on the markets.

If these fraudulent practices are discovered, it is the SEC in the United States that will take action. The cases they investigate and the penalties they impose are frequently publicized in the press. Additionally, the website of the SEC provides detailed information on such cases.

Possibly, the best-known fraud was The Great Salad Oil Swindle (Miller 1965).[1] To carry out such a scheme you only need to know that oil floats on top of water. The perpetrator, Tino DeAngelis, rented a petroleum tank farm in New Jersey. He was able to convince auditors, investors, and investment bankers that the tanks contained over $100 million in valuable vegetable oil. Indeed, independent auditors could easily check this claim using dipsticks that the tanks were full. Unfortunately, the tanks were mainly filled with water with a little vegetable oil floating on the surface to give a positive reading on the dipstick.

Another major case was the *Securities and Exchange Commission vs. Bristol-Myers Squibb Company* (SEC 2004).[2] The allegation by the SEC was that, from the first quarter of 2000 through the fourth quarter of 2001, Bristol-Myers was engaged in a fraudulent scheme to overstate its sales and earnings. The purpose of this was to make it appear that the company had met or exceeded financial projections set by the company's officers (targets) and earnings estimates established by Wall Street securities analysts.

There were two main methods adopted by Bristol-Myers. The first was stuffing its distribution channels with excess inventory near the end of every quarter in amounts sufficient to meet sales and earnings targets set by officers. In other words, the company was moving closing inventory from its own premises to distributors to make it appear as sales.

Second, the company improperly recognized about $1.5 billion in revenue from consignment-like sales associated with the channel-stuffing in violation of GAAP. At no time during 2000 or 2001 did Bristol-Myers disclose that: (1) it was artificially inflating its results through channel-stuffing; (2) channel-stuffing was contributing to a buildup in wholesaler inventory levels; (3) the buildup in wholesaler inventory posed a risk to Bristol-Myers's future sales and earnings; or (4) the company was using improper accounting, including cookie jar reserves, to further inflate its results. Cookie jar reserves is a way of putting aside funds in a prosperous year so that they can be used in a subsequent year to inflate profit. In March 2003, Bristol-Myers restated its prior financial statements and disclosed its channel-stuffing activities and improper accounting.

The next case exemplifies the comments we made earlier about recognizing revenue during the financial period in which it was actually earned. In 2002, the SEC alleged that between 1997 and 2000, Xerox employed several accounting maneuvers, to enhance its reported profits (SEC 2003).[3] The most significant was a change in which Xerox recorded revenue from copy-machine leases—recognizing a sale when a lease contract was signed, instead of recognizing revenue over the entire length of the contract. The dispute was not for the amount of total revenue, but for the financial periods to which it should have been allocated. At issue was when the revenue was recognized, not the validity of the revenue.

In response to SEC's complaint, Xerox Corporation neither admitted nor denied wrongdoing. However, it agreed to pay a $10 million penalty and to restate its financial results for the years 1997 through 2000.

Valuation of inventory is a fruitful area for fraud. The following example, brought forward by SEC in 2011, highlights the issue of valuing inventory (SEC 2011).[4] Point Blank Solutions (formerly DHB Industries) was a supplier to the U.S. Military. Unfortunately for Point Blank Solutions, the U.S. Army changed its specifications for hard armor plates for protective clothing. This meant that approximately $12.5 million of hard armor plates became obsolete. An additional $4.5 million of inventory became obsolete due to other changes including the discontinuation of certain vest fabrics and colors. The SEC claimed that the company failed to report that its inventory was obsolete and started overvaluing inventory in 2003. Two years later, the books were carrying inventory that was overvalued by $33 million.

A more recent case[5] is that of Monsanto which booked substantial amounts of revenue resulting from sales incentivized by a rebate program. The company delayed recognizing all of the related program costs at the same time because of issues with cost recognition. The SEC considered that the company materially misstated its consolidated earnings in corporate filings during a three-year period. This violated accounting rules and the SEC levied $80 million in penalties.

For those interested, the SEC website contains many examples of revenue and inventory frauds. Frequently, these manipulations are not detected for many years. The users of financial statements must be diligent and alert to warning signs such as:

- Increases in revenue figures when the general market is stagnant or declining;
- Closing inventory values increasing faster than revenues;
- Decreases in inventory turnover, that is, the amount of inventory held in relationship to the level of sales in the financial period;
- Inventory increasing as a percentage of total assets;
- Changes in the gross profit margin;
- A significant change in trends in sales or inventories over a period of time

## The Characteristics of National Accounting

The 1960s and 1970s attracted considerable interest in internationalizing accounting regulations. This interest led to attempts, mainly by academics, to identify the key factors or characteristics that formed the nature of a country's accounting regulations. Having identified the characteristics that shaped the standards, the next stage was to classify countries into groups of those sharing similar characteristics.

This classification of systems focused on the differences between country groups that were assumed to create potential barriers to internationalization (Mueller 1967, Frank 1979, Nair and Frank 1980, Nobes 1983[6]). One such classification that has remained relevant throughout the years is that based on a group of developed Western countries in the year 1980 (Nobes 1983).[7]

Figure 1.1 has been adapted from that research. Many of the terms identified in the diagram should be regarded as *loose labels*, which capture the attributes of the national accounting system.

There are two main classifications of the nature of accounting regulations in different countries. There are those countries where regulations are shaped by commercial factors and these are labeled as micro-fair-judgmental. The second classification is where regulations are prescribed mainly by government with the calculation of company tax being important and these are labeled as macro-uniform. The micro-judgmental classification is subdivided into Business Economics and Business Practice. The latter is further subdivided into UK influence and U.S. influence.

Of course, much has changed since 1980, both at the national level and at the international level. However, a similar study of eight countries has been made 30 years later. The results confirm that the classification by the IFRSs is similar to the classification of national practices drawn up in 1980, despite many years of pursuing harmonization.[8] The barriers to full internationalization of national accounting systems are discussed below.

### *Legal System*

Normally, countries either evolve or adopt one of the two legal systems. One is the common law system, which is developed on a case-by-case basis, with no general rules set out that could be used to resolve several different

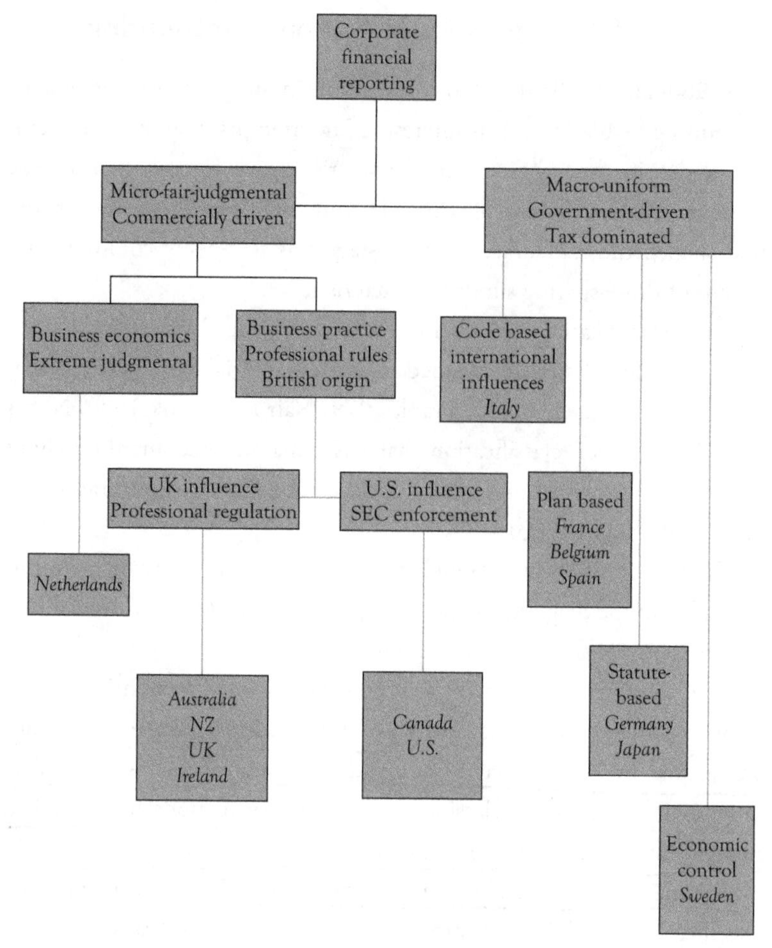


***Figure 1.1 Classification of global accounting systems***

*Source:* Adapted from Nobes (1983).

cases. Countries such as England, Singapore, and New Zealand have a common law system. Where a country has common law, accounting rules are not part of the law and are developed by the country's professional accounting bodies or some other form of standard setters.

In contrast, countries such as France, Portugal, and Japan have a code law system. Where there is a code law system, there is a wide set of rules to give guidance in all situations. Accounting regulations in these systems are often part of the law and controlled by the government either directly or indirectly.

### *Types of Business Organizations*

National accounting regulations address the different sources of finance obtained by a business, as well as its size and complexity in its country of operation. When they first start, businesses frequently obtain financing from the founders or owners. As companies grow larger, they cannot only rely on the existing owners of the company to invest more. Companies must seek external finance to fund that growth. The external finance can come from either individuals or organizations wishing to invest in the company, or financial institutions willing to lend money to the company.

In some countries, such as the United States, the United Kingdom, and Australia, the funding for companies has frequently come from individuals or groups. These shareholders make an investment in the company and, if the company is profitable, they receive a dividend and their share of the company grows in value. In such countries, there is often a powerful stock exchange that regulates some aspects of companies' activities. The shareholders are many in number and they are not able to demand specific financial information from companies for their own use. They must, therefore, rely on accounting regulations and stock exchange requirements to ensure that they receive financial statements that meet their needs.

Stock exchanges have strict regulations on the information to be publicly disclosed by a company it has "listed." Such companies must comply with accounting standards. These may be national accounting standards or, if a country has chosen to apply them, IFRSs. If a country has decided to adopt IFRSs, the stock exchanges in that country will require companies that are listed on it to comply with IFRSs. Usually, if the country has not adopted IFRS but retains national accounting standards the stock exchange will require companies listing on its stock exchange to comply with these.

The United States is somewhat different. The stock exchanges originally required foreign companies wishing to list to either submit financial statements that complied with U.S. standards or retain compliance with their own national standards and adjust these where there were differences between the requirements of the national standards and the U.S. standards. Rule changes passed in 2007 enable international companies to use IFRS reporting language in their filings instead of U.S. GAAP.

In 2016, the three largest stock exchanges, measured by number of companies listed, had the following number of companies.

| | |
|---|---|
| Bombay S.E. | 5,800 companies |
| New York Stock Exchange and NASDAQ | 5,300 companies |
| London Stock Exchange | 3,100 companies |

### *Tax Systems*

Countries have their own tax regulations for companies. In some countries, the tax rules dictate the way that the financial accounts are prepared. In other words, the financial statements are constructed in accordance with the tax legislation. The figures shown in the financial statements are the basis for the tax charge and, understandably, some companies may make decisions and present financial information in such a way as to lower their tax charge.

In other countries, the tax regulations are separated from the accounting regulations. Companies will prepare financial statements applying the accounting regulations and then adjustments will be made on the basis of the tax regulations to determine the amount of tax the company must pay. The two activities are therefore separated and the tax rules do not influence financial disclosures required by the accounting regulations.

### *The Accounting Profession*

In some countries, the accounting profession is very strong and involved in all aspects of corporate financial activities. Before the establishment of formal national accounting standard setters it was normally the accounting profession that issued advice to its members on the accepted accounting methods for business transactions (Table 1.1).

A highly developed accounting profession in a country will have a significant influence on the financial accounting regulations in that country. The members will sit on various committees, act as advisers, sponsor research, and publish papers on the correct way of accounting.

There is a concentration of accountants working for firms of auditors. These may be small firms offering a range of services to individuals,

*Table 1.1 The main accounting firms*

| Name of firm | Number of employees |
|---|---|
| Deloitte LLP | 244,000 (2017) |
| PwC | 223,000 (2016) |
| Ernst & Young LLP | 248,000 (2017) |
| KPMG | 189,000 (2016) |

including tax advice and auditing. The four largest firms have a massive presence and offer a complete range of services. The strength and influence of these firms are measured by the number of their employees.

### Culture

Culture is regarded as highly influential on the financial accounting and reporting system in a country, but it is difficult to define the direction and power of its influence. Research has classified countries according to cultural differences. A major influence was the theory that there are four dimensions along which cultural values can be analyzed: individualism–collectivism, uncertainty avoidance, power distance (strength of social hierarchy), and masculinity–femininity (task orientation versus person orientation).[9]

Many disciplines have applied the above theory, and the theoretical framework has been applied to develop a model that shows the relationships between cultural and accounting values.[10] The model did not operationalize the hypotheses or conduct any empirical tests, but several researchers have attempted to extend or refine this framework. The research has helped in understanding why differences in accounting regulations in a country may arise, but has not been of much help in resolving technical accounting issues.

However, in an increasingly globalized world, differences in national accounting cause problems. For companies, particularly multinational ones, it is expensive and complex to draw up different sets of accounts for the countries in which they operate. For investors, it is almost impossible to compare a company in one country with a similar company in another country.

Companies that conduct transactions with foreign suppliers and customers would find that a shared accounting language enhances ease of business and understanding. Investors, both large and small, need to be able to compare the financial statements of companies in different countries. For international capital markets to operate efficiently and effectively financial information from different companies in various countries needs to be comparable.

## Accounting Regulations in the United States

The formation of the SEC can be traced back to the 1930s. The stock market collapse in 1929 destroyed public confidence in the financial markets. It has been contended that, among other factors, one reason for the crash was the poor state of economic intelligence (Galbraith 2009).[11] Investors, both large and small, banks, and financial institutions lost great sums of money. There was a consensus that for the economy to recover, the public's faith in the capital markets needed to be restored. It fell to Congress to identify the problems and recommend solutions.

In 1933, the Securities Act was passed and this was followed in 1934 by the Securities Exchange Act. The latter created the SEC, a formidable body with significant powers. Its task was to restore investor confidence in the capital markets by providing investors and the markets with more reliable financial information and clear rules of honest dealing.

Our interest is the role of the SEC in ensuring that companies publicly offering securities to investors must disclose to the public the truth about their businesses, the securities they are selling, and the risks involved in investing. To achieve this, the SEC requires public companies to disclose meaningful financial and other information to the public. These disclosures provide a base of knowledge for all investors to decide whether to buy, sell, or hold a particular security. Only through the steady flow of timely, comprehensive, and accurate information can people make sound investment decisions.

Although the focus of SEC is on public companies, it determines what may be regarded as *good accounting*. This establishes a perspective that influences the accounting used in private companies.

### *The Securities and Exchange Commission*

One characteristic of SEC is the size of the organization. It has approximately 3,500 staff located in Washington, DC, and 11 regional offices throughout the country. The agency's functional responsibilities are organized into 5 divisions and 23 offices, each of which is headquartered in Washington, DC. The SEC is responsible for:

1. Interpreting and enforcing federal securities law
2. Issuing new rules and amending existing rules
3. Overseeing the inspection of securities firms, brokers, investment advisers, and ratings agencies
4. Overseeing private regulatory organizations in the securities, accounting, and auditing fields
5. Coordinating U.S. securities regulation with federal, state, and foreign authorities

The Commission holds meetings that are open to the public and the news media unless the discussion is about confidential matters, such as whether to begin an enforcement investigation.

Critical to the SEC's effectiveness is its enforcement authority. Each year, the SEC brings hundreds of civil enforcement actions against individuals and companies for the violation of the securities laws. The main types of activities that lead to an SEC investigation are:

1. Misrepresentation or omission of important information about securities
2. Manipulating the market prices of securities
3. Stealing customers' funds or securities; violating broker-dealers' responsibility to treat customers fairly
4. Insider trading (violating a trust relationship by trading while in possession of material, nonpublic information about a security)
5. Selling unregistered securities

The statistics from 2011 to October 7, 2016[12] demonstrate the scope of the SEC's enforcement activities (Table 1.2).

Every SEC investigation is conducted privately. Informal inquiry may be conducted by interviewing witnesses, examining brokerage records, reviewing trading data, and other methods. With a formal order of investigation, witnesses can be compelled by subpoena to testify and produce

*Table 1.2 The SEC's enforcement activities*

| | |
|---|---|
| Number of entities and individuals charged | 204 |
| Number of CEOs, CFOs, and other senior corporate officers charged | 93 |
| Number of individuals who have received officer and director bars, industry bars, or commission suspensions | 54 |
| Penalties ordered or agreed to | $1.93 billion |
| Disgorgement and prejudgment interest ordered or agreed to | $1.47 billion |
| Additional monetary relief obtained for harmed investors | $418 million* |
| Total penalties, disgorgement, and other monetary relief | $3.76 billion |

*In settlements with Evergreen, J.P. Morgan, State Street, TD Ameritrade, and Claymore Advisors.
*Source:* https://www.sec.gov/spotlight/enf-actions-fc.shtml.

books, records, and other relevant documents. After reviewing the findings, the SEC can authorize the staff to file a case in federal court or bring an administrative action. In many cases, the SEC and the party charged may decide to settle the matter without trial.

An SEC filing is a formal document that the SEC requires from certain groups and individuals. There are many such documents depending on the circumstances. Those companies with securities that are publicly traded are required to disclose information on an ongoing basis.

Public companies (other than small business issuers) are obliged to submit annual reports on Form 10-K, quarterly reports on Form 10-Q, and current reports on Form 8-K for a number of specified events and must comply with a variety of other disclosure requirements. The Form 10-K, which should be filed with the SEC, contains very detailed information about the company's financial activities for the year.

At one time, companies were required to file their Form 10-K within 90 days of their financial year end. There have been some adjustments to the regulations but the current position is shown in Table 1.3.

The SEC has developed categories depending on the size of the company. The size is determined by the public float of a company, which is the portion of shares held by public investors opposed to locked-in stock held by promoters, company officers, controlling-interest investors, or government. Large accelerated filers are companies with at least $700 million in public float, while accelerated filers are companies with at least $75 million but less than $700 million in public float. The final

*Table 1.3 Deadlines for filing periodic reports*

| Category | Form 10-K (days) | Form 10-Q (days) |
|---|---|---|
| Large accelerated filer | 60 | 40 |
| Accelerated filers | 75 | 40 |
| Nonaccelerated filers | 90 | 45 |

group consists of the nonaccelerated filers. These are listed companies that have a public float under $75 million or fail to meet other criteria for an "accelerated filer." The present deadlines (SEC 2014b)[13] for filing for these three groups are shown in above Table 1.3.

The SEC has adopted a system of disclosure rules for smaller companies filing periodic reports and registration statements with the SEC. The rules are scaled to reflect the characteristics and needs of smaller companies and their investors.

The *smaller reporting company* category includes all companies that enter the public reporting system with less than $75 million in common equity public float. Companies' eligibility for smaller reporting company status is based on the last business day of their most recent second fiscal quarter.

Smaller reporting companies prepare and file their SEC reports and registration statements with the same forms as other SEC-reporting companies, though the information required to be disclosed may differ. A new Article 8 of Regulation S-X contains the SEC requirements for financial statements, while Regulation S-K contains the nonfinancial disclosure requirements. To locate the scaled disclosure requirements in Regulation S-K, smaller reporting companies will refer to the special paragraphs labeled *smaller reporting companies* in Regulation S-K.

The SEC has immense authority in ensuring compliance with U.S. GAAP. One could argue that the reason for the formation of the SEC is the reason that U.S. GAAP has developed in the way that it has. The actual work of setting accounting regulations, however, falls on the next body we discuss, the FASB.

### The Financial Accounting Standards Board

The FASB was founded in 1973 following the recommendations of the 1972 Wheat Committee of the American Institute of Certified Public

Accountants (AICPA). The FASB was a different type of organization from its predecessor, the Accounting Principles Board (APB), which was controlled by the accounting profession. The FASB was to be accountable to the SEC and had the responsibility of acting in the best interests of the main financial statement users, deemed to be investors. As we will see later in this book, the selection of the investor as the main user causes problems when international accounting is debated.

The FASB is authorized by the SEC. This is an unusual relationship as the FASB is a private-sector organization but under the careful surveillance of the SEC. The accounting standards issued by the FASB are recognized as authoritative and generally accepted for purposes of U.S. federal securities laws.

SFASs were issued by the FASB for more than 30 years and were intended specifically for listed companies. However, their influence was much wider. Small businesses also have people interested in their financial affairs: the owners, tax collectors, banks, and any other party who is owed money. Although they do not directly fall under the accounting regulations of the FASB, those standards established what is considered common practice.

**Statement of Financial Accounting Standard**

A formal document that sets out detailed accounting, reporting, and disclosure requirements. SFASs are issued with the expectation that all reporting companies listed on American stock exchanges will adhere to them.

In 2009, the FASB ASC was launched and now FASB Accounting Standards Updates (ASUs) are issued to amend the codification. The FASB is part of a structure that is independent of all other business and professional organizations. This independent role is essential for the way that it operates. The structure includes the following organizations.

### Financial Accounting Foundation

The Foundation is the independent, private-sector organization that is responsible for the oversight, administration, and finances of the FASB, the Government Accounting Standards Board (GASB), and their advisory councils Financial Accounting Standards Advisory Council (FASAC) and Government Accounting Standards Advisory Council (GASAC). The Foundation's primary duties include protecting the independence and integrity of the standards-setting process and appointing members of the FASB, GASB, FASAC, and GASAC.

### Financial Accounting Standards Advisory Council

The primary function of FASAC is to advise the FASB on technical issues on the Board's agenda, possible new agenda items, project priorities, procedural matters that may require the attention of the FASB, and other matters as may be requested by the FASB or its chairman. At present, the Council has more than 30 members who represent a broad cross-section of the FASB's constituency.

### Government Accounting Standards Board

The GASB was established in 1984 to set standards of financial accounting and reporting for state and local governmental units. As with the FASB, the Foundation is responsible for selecting its members, ensuring adequate funding, and exercising general oversight.

### Government Accounting Standards Advisory Council

The GASAC has the responsibility for advising the GASB on technical issues on the Board's agenda, project priorities, matters likely to require the attention of the GASB, and such other matters as may be requested by the GASB or its chairman.

There are seven full-time members of the FASB. The members are appointed for five-year terms and are eligible for reappointment to one additional five-year term. On their appointment, they must sever any existing connections with their current firms or institutions to ensure their independence.

The Board is assisted by a staff of more than 60 professionals who have knowledge and experience in investing, accounting, finance, business, accounting education, and research. The staff works directly with the

Board and project resource groups, conducts research, participates in round-table meetings, analyzes oral and written comments received from the public, and prepares recommendations and drafts of documents for consideration by the Board.

Further support is given to the Board and staff by four advisory groups. These groups share their knowledge and experience with the Board on projects on the Board's agenda, possible new agenda items, practice and implementation of new standards, and strategic and other matters. Information provided by advisory group members is communicated to the Board in a variety of ways, including public advisory meetings and comment letters. Currently, the groups are:

- FASAC
- Investor Advisory Committee (IAC)
- Not-for-Profit Advisory Committee (NAC)
- Small Business Advisory Committee (SBAC)

### *The FASB Standards-Setting Process*

The process will depend on the nature and scope of the reporting issues involved. For complex subjects the process can take several years. However, the main stages are as follows:

1. The Board identifies financial reporting issues based on requests or recommendations from stakeholders or through other means. As we work through subsequent chapters we will examine some of these issues.
2. The FASB chairman decides whether to add a project to the technical agenda, after consultation with FASB members and others as appropriate, and subject to oversight by the Foundation's Board of Trustees.
3. The Board deliberates, at one or more public meetings, the reporting issues identified and analyzed by the staff.
4. The Board issues an Exposure Draft (ED) to solicit broad stakeholder input. (In some projects, the Board may issue a Discussion Paper (DP) to obtain input in the project's early stages.) EDs and DPs are

an integral part of most standard setters including the International Accounting Standards Board (IASB).

5. The Board holds a public round-table meeting on the ED, if necessary.
6. The staff analyzes comment letters, public round-table discussion, and any other information obtained through due process activities. The Board redeliberates the proposed provisions, carefully considering the stakeholder input received, at one or more public meetings.
7. At this stage, it may be necessary to issue a revised ED incorporating the comments that have been received.
8. The Board issues an ASU describing amendments to the ASC.

The last point above introduces a significant change in the procedures of the FASB. From 1973 to 2009, the FASB issued 168 SFASs. Following a major five-year project, the FASB ASC was launched on July 1, 2009. From that date FASB ASUs are issued to amend the codification. Updates are published for all authoritative U.S. GAAP released by the FASB, regardless of the form in which such guidance may have been issued prior to the release of the FASB codification (e.g., FASB Statements, Emerging Issues Task Force (EITF) Abstracts, FASB Staff Positions, and so on). Updates will also be issued for amendments to the SEC content in the FASB codification, as well as for editorial changes.

The FASB ASC is now the official source of authoritative, nongovernmental GAAP (also known as U.S. GAAP). When it was introduced the codification did not change U.S. GAAP as it was, but ordered and structured thousands of pronouncements issued by the FASB, the AICPA, and other standards-setting bodies into roughly 90 accounting topics. It also includes relevant SEC guidance that follows the same topical structure in separate sections in the codification.

The structure of the codification is in three tiers. Each *Topic* contains at least one *Subtopic* containing *Sections* that include the actual accounting guidance. Sections are based on the nature of the content (e.g., scope, recognition, measurement, and so on) and are standardized throughout the codification. Each Section includes numbered Paragraphs commencing with the Section number followed by the unique paragraph number. For example, in Section 20 the first paragraph is numbered 20.1.

New additions to U.S. GAAP are issued by means of a FASB document called an ASU. These bring changes in the ASC and therefore in U.S. GAAP. A useful guide to the codification system has been published by PricewaterhouseCoopers and this was updated in 2017 (PwC).[14]

### *Financial Information Available*

We noted earlier that the SEC requires publicly traded companies to file specific documents to cover different periods of time. A fiscal or financial year is a period for calculating the annual (yearly) financial statements. In many countries, regulatory laws regarding accounting and taxation require such reports once every 12 months, but do not require that the period reported on constitutes a calendar year (i.e., January 1 to December 31).

Some companies choose to end their fiscal year on the same day of the week, such a day being the one closest to a particular date. However, the fiscal year is identical to the calendar year for about 65 percent of publicly traded companies in the United States and for a majority of large companies in the United Kingdom.

The date a company chooses as its year end may be important if there has been a recent change in accounting regulations. Given that word of caution, the amount of information that a publicly traded company makes available can be overwhelming and takes many forms.

#### Form 10-K

The annual report on Form 10-K provides a comprehensive overview of the company's business and financial condition as well as audited financial statements. Although similarly named, the annual report on Form 10-K is distinct from the *annual report to shareholders,* which a company must send to its shareholders when it holds an annual general meeting to elect directors.

Form 10-K is a lengthy document and the main sections are:

*Part I*

ITEM 1. Description of Business
ITEM 1A. Risk Factor
ITEM 1B. Unresolved Staff Comments

ITEM 2. Description of Properties
ITEM 3. Legal Proceedings
ITEM 4. Mine Safety Disclosures
ITEM 5. Market for Registrant's Common Equity, Related Stockholder Matters, and Issuer Purchases of Equity Securities
ITEM 6. Selected Financial Data
ITEM 7. Management's Discussion and Analysis of Financial Condition and Results of Operations
ITEM 7A. Quantitative and Qualitative Disclosures about Market Risk
ITEM 8. Financial Statements and Supplementary Data
ITEM 9. Changes in and Disagreements with Accountants on Accounting and Financial Disclosure
ITEM 9A (T). Controls and Procedures
ITEM 9B. Other Information
ITEM 10. Directors, Executive Officers, and Corporate Governance
ITEM 11. Executive Compensation
ITEM 12. Security Ownership of Certain Beneficial Owners and Management and Related Stockholder Matters
ITEM 13. Certain Relationships and Related Transactions, and Director Independence
ITEM 14. Principal Accounting Fees and Services
ITEM 15. Exhibits, Financial Statement Schedules Signatures

Companies must produce their financial statements within a restricted time period. All the information needed to do so will not always be available; therefore, estimates are needed. These estimates are always drawn to the attention of the reader and an example is shown below.

> The preparation of consolidated financial statements in conformity with U.S. Generally Accepted Accounting Principles (GAAP) requires us to make estimates and assumptions that affect the amounts reported and disclosed in the financial statements and the accompanying notes. Actual results could differ materially from these estimates. On an ongoing basis, we evaluate our estimates, including those related to the accounts receivable and sales

> allowances, fair values of financial instruments, intangible assets and goodwill, useful lives of intangible assets and property and equipment, income taxes, and contingent liabilities, among others. We base our estimates on historical experience and on various other assumptions that are believed to be reasonable, the results of which form the basis for making judgments about the carrying values of assets and liabilities. (p. 47)

Note: Google changed from filing under "Google" to filing under "Alphabet" in 2016.
*Source:* Google Form 10-K for the year ended December 31, 2016.

All companies, foreign and domestic, are required to file registration statements, periodic reports, and other forms electronically through the Electronic Data-Gathering, Analysis, and Retrieval (EDGAR) system. Anyone can access and download information from the system for free. Here you will find links to a complete list of filings available through EDGAR and instructions for searching the EDGAR database (www.sec.gov/edgar/aboutedgar.htm).

## Annual Reports

Companies must send annual reports to their shareholders. Under the proxy rules as set out by the SEC, reporting companies are required to post their proxy materials, including their annual reports, on their company websites. Companies sometimes elect to send their Form 10-K to their shareholders in lieu of providing shareholders with an annual report. Some companies may submit their annual reports electronically in the SEC's EDGAR database.

The annual report to shareholders is the main method adopted by most public companies to disclose corporate information to their shareholders. It is normally a state-of-the-company report, including an opening letter from the CEO, financial data, the results of continuing operations, market segment information, new product plans, subsidiary activities, and research and development activities on future programs.

Such a document can be lengthy; Ford's Motor Company fiscal year 2016 report, for example, runs to 200 pages. This is significantly larger than the 161 pages for Ford we included in the first edition of this book and it is by no means the largest company annual report available. Below we show the listing for part 2 of the Ford 2016 report.

**Part II**

Item 5 Market for Common Equity, Related Stockholder Matters and Issuer Purchases of Equity Securities
Item 6 Selected Financial Data
Item 7 Management's Discussion and Analysis of Financial Condition and Results of Operations
Overview
Results of Operations—2016
Automotive Segment
Financial Services Segment
All Other
Special Items
Taxes
Results of Operations—2015
Automotive Segment
Financial Services Segment
All Other
Special Items
Taxes
Liquidity and Capital Resources
Credit Ratings
2017 Industry and GDP Planning Assumptions
Production Volumes
Outlook
Non-GAAP Financial Measure Reconciliations
2016 Supplemental Financial Information
Critical Accounting Estimates
Accounting Standards Issued But Not Yet Adopted
Aggregate Contractual Obligations
Item 7A Quantitative and Qualitative Disclosures About Market Risk
Item 8 Financial Statements and Supplementary Data
Item 9 Changes in and Disagreements with Accountants on Accounting and Financial Disclosure
Item 9A Controls and Procedures
Item 9B Other Information

*Source:* Financial information contained herein (pages 23–100) is excerpted from the Annual Report on Form 10-K for the year ended December 31, 2016 of Ford Motor Company.

This report conveys a substantial amount of information. A detailed explanation of all of the items listed is beyond our scope but the seventh item from the end refers to "Accounting Standards Issued but Not

Yet Adopted." This underpins a point made previously that, although a standard may be published, it does not necessarily mean that it has become operative. Ford, as with most companies, refers to those standards that they have not followed because they are not yet operative.

### *Reliability of Information*

The reliability of the financial information provided by companies is only as good as the accounting regulations requiring it, assuming that the company is in compliance with regulations. We have referred to the estimates and assumptions that companies are compelled to make because of the necessity to issue financial statements for a period of time, even if all of the information is not available.

Our confidence in accounting regulations and the financial information provided by companies is enhanced by the Auditor's Report. All publicly traded companies will have external auditors who will examine the accounting processes and procedures of the company. Their opinion will be given in conjunction with the financial statements. Remember that, as shown in the following example from General Motors, it is the responsibility of the company's management to prepare the financial statements.

> In our opinion, the consolidated financial statements referred to above present fairly, in all material respects, the financial position of General Motors Company and subsidiaries as of December 31, 2016 and 2015, and the results of their operations and their cash flows for each of the three years in the period ended December 31, 2016, in conformity with accounting principles generally accepted in the United States of America. Also, in our opinion, the Company maintained, in all material respects, effective internal control over financial reporting as of December 31, 2016, based on the criteria established in *Internal Control—Integrated Framework (2013)* issued by the Committee of Sponsoring Organizations of the Treadway Commission.
>
> *Source:* http://corporate.ford.com/our-company/investors/reports-financial-information/annual-reports.

## Conclusion

It has taken the United States almost 100 years from the position of public companies having no requirement to publish financial information to a substantial amount of corporate financial information being freely available. Financial information disclosure itself has not been the only achievement: a system of regulation has been formed to ensure that companies have a framework by which to prepare and present their financial data.

The SEC is, in all probability, one of the most powerful bodies in the world with the responsibilities of ensuring U.S. public companies disclose meaningful financial and other information to the public. To do so, it requires a body to set out accounting regulations rather than allow individual companies to apply their own concepts and assumptions. The FASB has been established in the role of standard setter.

Most countries have a body responsible for setting accounting standards. Other countries do not necessarily follow, or even agree with, U.S. accounting regulations and instead follow their own methods. This has become a major problem as businesses have become global in their operations. Is the company you are trading within Germany as financially solid as you believe? Will your investments in apparently highly profitable foreign companies prove as financially rewarding as you hoped?

In the next chapter, we explain the growth of international accounting and how approximately 150 jurisdictions (with the exception of the United States) have implemented accounting regulations that comply with, or are substantially based on, IFRSs. We examine the IASB, the organization that sets the international standards, and the process for issuing these standards.

# CHAPTER 2

# The Move to International Accounting

## About This Chapter

Although the United States had implemented a procedure for rigorous accounting regulations within its own borders, one serious problem arose. As business became more international, the issue of countries developing their own, unique accounting standards became apparent. The financial statements of a company in one country could not be compared to that from another country as the rules in drawing them up were different. If a foreign company wished to be listed on the New York Stock Exchange (NYSE), it would either have to do reconciliation with U.S. Generally Accepted Accounting Principles (GAAP) or draw up new financial statements complying with U.S. GAAP.

It did not make sense that countries' accounting regulations were different and it was confusing when operating at the international level. One solution was that all countries should use U.S. accounting standards. An alternative approach was to establish an international body that would be responsible for issuing standards. As it was apparent that some countries would be reluctant to abandon their own standards for those determined by the United States, an international standard setting body appeared to be the only viable option.

It is frequently easier to determine the best way to make progress and more difficult to put it into action. If we are to have international accounting standards (IASs), an organization must be formed to develop these standards. Funding will be required and the agreement of countries to comply with the standards.

In this chapter, we examine the problems of national accounting standards and the factors that operated to give a country its own particular form of accounting regulations. We describe the background to the formation of the International Accounting Standards Committee (IASC). This body issued IASs commencing with IAS 1 Presentation of Financial Statements and ending with IAS 41 Agriculture. Many of the standards issued are still in operation.

After several years the IASC was succeeded by the International Accounting Standards Board (IASB). This body retained all the IASs that had been issued. It also continues to issue regulations but name them International Financial Reporting Standards (IFRSs). It commenced with IFRS 1 First Time Adoption of International Financial Reporting Standards and in 2016 issued IFRS 16 Leases.

We complete this chapter by looking at the progress toward international accounting. We examine the adoption of some countries, such as Australia, Canada, and the countries in the European Union that have adopted international standards. We also examine the move toward international accounting in countries such as China, India, and Japan. The progress of the United States toward converging with international standards and its retreat from that aim is left to Chapters 3 and 4.

## The Problems of National Accounting

As can be seen from the explanations in the previous chapter, the demands and pressures of national, political, and economic environments largely formed the route that countries followed to establish their own standard-setting bodies. The structure, operation, and authority of the national standard setters are shaped within existing national practices and conventions.

Standard setters work within a coalition of interests, including reporting organizations, shareholders, the media, and political groups. The powers of these interested parties differ, and the need and desire of the accounting standard setters to gain the support of these particular factions also vary. For example, the United States is notable because of the considerable statutory authority of the Securities and Exchange Commission (SEC) to participate in the standard-setting process and the extent to which lobbying takes place.

Given the unique histories of national accounting standards development in each country, it is not surprising that there are significant differences in their specific accounting regulations. In the early years of the 20th century, there seemed to be little need for countries to discuss with each other how accounting standards should be formulated and applied. However, opinions were to change.

The creation of the European Union highlighted the problems. The different countries in Europe had different accounting systems. This made it difficult for conducting trading operations and cross-border investment. The European Commission started to tackle this issue in the 1970s. Several directives were issued with which all EU countries were compelled to comply. The purpose of the directives was to make financial statements more comparable in terms of presentation, format, and measurement, which were implemented by all EU members by 1991.

There were also changes taking place in the United States. In the latter half of the 20th century, there were some highly publicized examples of very profitable companies in Europe that wanted to list shares on the NYSE. In order to do so, the profitable company had to redraft those financial statements in accordance with U.S. GAAP. In some instances, the previously declared profit for a financial year turned into a loss due to the application of different accounting standards.

## The Classic Case

Possibly the most famous case is that of Daimler Benz AG, a German company that wished to list its shares on the U.S. Stock Exchange in the early 1990s. To do so, it had to reconcile the profit it had shown for 1993, which was prepared in accordance with German GAAP, with what the profit would have been if the company had adopted U.S. GAAP. The net income, or profit, the company had reported in its German financial statements was DM615 million. After the company had made all the adjustments to comply with U.S. GAAP the reported net income turned to a net loss of DM1839 million.

This significant difference in the financial results of Daimler Benz demonstrated that accounting regulations at the national level did not make sense when viewed from an international perspective. It is reasonable to question how a company can make a profit under one set of accounting rules but this turns into a loss when other rules are applied. Which rules are the correct ones? Accounting regulations needed to be changed, but the question was how this could be achieved.

In the following sections we provide an answer to this dilemma. We describe the development of international accounting regulations and the gradual involvement of various countries.

## The International Accounting Standards Committee

The IASC was founded in 1973 by the accountancy bodies, not the governments, of nine countries: Australia, Canada, France, Germany, Japan, Mexico, the Netherlands, the United Kingdom and Ireland (UK), and the United States. It was established as a private sector nongovernment organization (NGO) with a part-time body of standard setters who met three or four times a year in cities around the globe. The organization was based in London, with a small, full-time secretariat. At this point in the chapter, it is worth mentioning that the IASB is still based in London, although its formal meetings are held in various countries.

The objectives of the IASC were:

- To formulate and publish, in the public interest, accounting standards to be observed in the presentation of financial statements and to promote their worldwide acceptance and observance;
- To work generally for the improvement and harmonization of regulations, accounting standards, and procedures relating to the presentation of financial statements.

The above objectives were extremely ambitious for an organization that was resourced very modestly and had no enforcement powers. The IASC intended to achieve these objectives by:

- Ensuring that published financial statements comply with IASs in all material respects;
- Persuading governments and standard-setting bodies that published financial statements comply with IASs;

- Persuading authorities controlling securities markets and the industrial and business community that published financial statements comply with IASs.

It is important to emphasize that the IASC was not established primarily to promote the growth of international capital markets. The reverse was the case and it was the increasing globalization of markets and business that led to increasing pressure for IASs to promote comparability.

Although the IASC made considerable progress, it had a number of weaknesses that meant that it was less effective than was required. Its main problems were:

1. Too many of its standards allowed alternative choices in accounting treatment and were open to different interpretations. This allowed flexibility in drawing up corporate financial reports, thus allowing countries and companies to claim to be following IASs but still draw up financial statements that were not fully comparable.
2. The IASC did not have enforcement powers or mechanisms to obtain compliance. Thus, consensus could only be achieved by issuing standards containing sufficient flexibility to obtain widespread acceptance.
3. There were structural and resource problems that the IASC could not remedy. The members of the IASC were from national professional accounting bodies. Many of these had no responsibility for standard setting in their own countries, thus reducing IASC's ability to influence and persuade national standard setters.
4. There was the question of how much independence the IASC needed from the professional accounting bodies to conduct its activities. The technical contribution of the professional accounting bodies was essential but was regarded by some as placing the IASC in the direct influence of one particular interest group. There were other interest groups represented, for example, analysts and academics, but professional accounting bodies were perceived as dominant. To some extent, this perceived dominance also weakened the possibility of achieving a mechanism for enforcement. Few would wish to allow

professional accounting bodies, however well intentioned, to make the regulations for worldwide accounting as well as having the power to enforce them.

Although interest was expressed in making progress in internationalization, the major national economies were still relying on national accounting standards. It was the smaller countries that tended to adopt international standards. The question whether the IASC could achieve its goal of being truly international still remained. Either a complete overhaul of all aspects of the IASC was required or a new body needed to be formed. The latter was the course of action chosen.

## The International Accounting Standards Board

The IASB was established formally in April 2001 with the following objectives:

- Developing in the public interest, a single set of high-quality, understandable, and enforceable global accounting standards;
- Helping participants in the world's capital markets and other users make economic decisions by having access to high-quality, transparent, and comparable information;
- Promoting the use and vigorous application of those standards;
- Bringing about convergence of national accounting standards and IASs to high-quality solutions.

The IASB "adopted" the IASs issued by the IASC and commenced issuing its own standards entitled IFRSs. It has a technical role of setting standards. It has no authority to compel companies to adopt standards, to monitor their compliance, or to take action to remedy practices with which it disagrees. National governments determine whether they will adopt IFRSs.

Its structure of the IFRS Foundation is displayed in Figure 2.1.

The IFRS foundation monitoring board was created in January 2009. The Board is responsible for approving appointment of trustees and ensuring that they discharge their duties. The IFRS Foundation Trustees is responsible for governance and funding. It is the oversight body of the

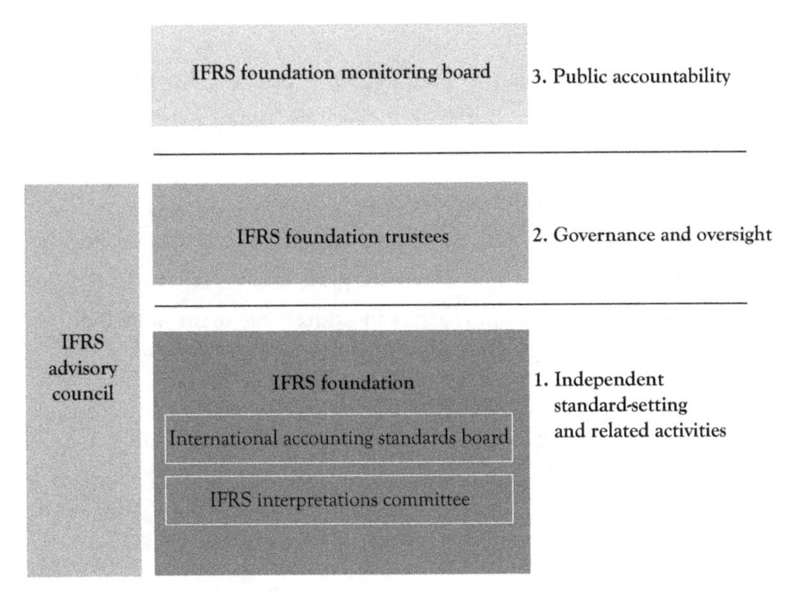


*Figure 2.1 The IFRS foundation*

IASB. The IFRS advisory council gives advice to both the trustees and the IASB. Its members consist of analysts, preparers, and academics. These are appointed by the Trustees.

The role of the IFRS Interpretations Committee (IFRIC) is a crucial one. It examines newly identified financial reporting issues not specifically dealt with in IFRSs and issues where unsatisfactory or conflicting interpretations have developed, or seem likely to develop in the absence of authoritative guidance. IFRIC interpretations are subject to IASB approval and have the same authority as a standard issued by the IASB.

Not all of the issues brought to the Committee will lead to an interpretation. The committee may decide to pass the issue to the IASB or that the standard does not require any interpretation. The committee does not give advice to individual companies and firms of accountants who may have difficulties in understanding a particular standard.

Our interest is focused on the IASB, the body responsible for issuing IFRSs. The process in issuing a standard has the following six stages:

1. Establishing an agenda
   The IASB evaluates the merits of adding a potential item to its agenda, mainly by reference to the needs of investors.

2. Planning the project
   In developing a plan to conduct the work, the Board will decide whether to conduct the work by itself or jointly with another standard setting body.
3. Issuing a Discussion Paper (DP)
   It is normal practice for the Board to issue a DP and ask for comments. In issuing a DP, the Board gives a comprehensive review of the issues, possible approaches in addressing them, and their own preliminary views.
4. Publishing the Exposure Draft (ED)
   The ED is the IASB's main vehicle for consulting the public. The ED sets out a specific proposal in the form of a proposed standard (or amendment to an existing standard).
5. Publishing the standard
   The Board has to decide whether to publish revised proposals for comments as a second ED or whether to proceed to issuing a standard. When the IASB is satisfied that it has reached a conclusion on the issues arising from the ED, it instructs the staff to draft the IFRS.
6. Implementation of the standard
   After an IFRS is issued, the staff and the IASB members hold regular meetings with interested parties, including other standard-setting bodies, to help understand unanticipated issues related to the practical implementation and potential impact of its proposals.

This is an exhaustive, time-consuming process. Not only is there input from the two advisory bodies, but at the DP and ED stages, there is opportunity for the public to make comments and suggestions. All of this documentation, including copies of the comment letters, is available on the IFRS website.

Once issued, standards may subsequently be revised if there are changes in business practices or deficiencies in the standard. If the issues are extensive, the existing standard may be withdrawn and a new standard with a new IFRS number issued. In addition to these major changes, the IASB annually conducts an improvement project, which may make minor amendments to some standards.

As far as the present standards themselves are concerned, there is some confusion because of the change of names and the apparent duplication of some individual standards. The IASC issued 41 standards between 1975 and 2000. The standards were numbered consecutively starting with 1 and each standard also had a descriptive title; for example, IAS 7 Cash Flow Statements. Most of the IASC standards are still in force.

When the IASB took over from the IASC, it adopted the IASs that were still in force and started to add its own standards, which were titled IFRS. Once again these standards are numbered consecutively, starting with 1, and have a descriptive title, such as IFRS 3 Business Combinations.

When referring to the issued standards, either the term IASs or IFRSs is used. It is essential, however, to attach correctly the term IAS or IFRS when referring to a specific standard, for example, IAS 2 Inventories or IFRS 2 Share-Based Payment. In this book we use the term International Standards to mean both IASs and IFRSs.

The IASB has made substantial progress with the acceptance of international standards. It is claimed that there are more than 100 jurisdictions that have adopted international standards. However, caution should be expressed about the rigor and extent of that adoption. In some instances, the adoption is partial, with only certain types of organizations in a particular country compelled to comply with the international standards. We examine this issue when we consider certain countries at the end of this chapter.

A few countries maintain that their standards are similar to and are based on international standards, but this does not mean that there is full compliance. A list of countries that claim to have adopted international standards and the scope are given on the IAS Plus website (http://www.iasplus.com/en/jurisdictions).

Two research papers that have investigated the characteristics of adopting and nonadopting companies have arrived at interesting conclusions.

The first paper examined 102 non-EU countries.[1] The researchers found that more powerful countries are less likely to adopt IFRS and suggested that they are reluctant to surrender standard-setting authority to an international body. This is pertinent to the United States where the SEC has the ultimate authority for accounting regulations. The researchers also found that a country is more likely to adopt IFRS if its trade partners or countries within its geographical region are IFRS adopters.

A later study took a different perspective and examined how standards were accepted and implemented.[2] Their sample included 183 nations around the world. They gave significant focus to the 25 largest nations according to the gross national product. They concluded that the probability of assuring strict implementation of accounting and reporting standards may be affected by weak national cultural ethics, unstable authoritarian forms of government, and economic power measured by high debt levels and rapid growth rates.

Of course, adoption is only one part of the process and for standards to be effective, some form of monitoring and enforcement is required. The IASB does not have direct powers or procedures to ensure companies in individual countries comply with international standards, but national mechanisms may already be in operation or are being created. The IASB, however, has to rely on the mechanisms in place in individual countries to ensure enforcement.

### *Enforcement Mechanisms*

The first stage of monitoring for compliance with international standards is within the company where control systems, including internal audit, can ensure that standards are applied. The commitment of management is also required to ensure that financial statements fairly represent the financial performance and position of the organization.

A second stage in ensuring compliance with international standards is an audit conducted by an auditor who is deemed to be independent of the company. An audit will involve an examination of the procedures, processes, and records of the company, and the financial statements that are drawn from those records. The auditor will express an opinion on those financial statements in a standard audit report.

There are different national rules on the status of organizations that require an external audit. At a minimum, an external audit is normally required by those companies whose shares are listed on a stock exchange and the auditors are reporting their opinion to the shareholders.

The specific duties performed by an external auditor will normally be set out in the contract with the company. The auditors will be expected:

- To ensure that all the necessary information and explanations for the audit have been obtained.

- To ensure that proper books of accounts have been kept and maintained by the organization.
- To confirm that the accounts dealt with in the report are in agreement with the books of accounts and are in conformity with national regulations.
- To issue an auditor's report that should contain a clear written expression of opinion on the financial statements taken as a whole.

It is not the normal duty of an auditor to conduct a fraud investigation. Unfortunately, research indicates that there are important differences in the understanding between auditors and users of the purpose of the audit and the meanings of statements made in the audit report.[3] One misunderstanding that appears in most countries is that users of financial statements mostly believe that auditors search for fraud and financial manipulations. That is not the case, although if they encounter such practices the auditors should report them.

The final and critical stage is the monitoring and enforcement mechanism held by a regulator. There are models currently employed at the national level. There are security commissions, such as the SEC in the United States, stock exchanges that can delist companies for regulatory transgressions, and other national bodies that have some legal support.

### *Funding*

The funding of the work of the IASB comes through the IFRS Foundation. This is a not-for-profit organization whose primary source of income comes from contributions from jurisdictions that have put in place international financing regimes. Contributions that come from other sources and the international accounting firms are the most significant source of support.

Since the commencement of the convergence project, the United States has been a major contributor as a country, usually ranking in the top three donations from all countries. In Table 2.1, we show the annual contributions from the United States for the period 2008–2016. All contributions are translated into sterling on the date they are received.

It is noticeable that the contributions from the United States have been declining steadily since 2010 apart from the spike in 2014. This increase

*Table 2.1 U.S. contributions to the IFRS foundation*

| Date | U.S. contribution |
|---|---|
| 2008 | £1,891,474 |
| 2009 | £1,846,698 |
| 2010 | £1,897,808 |
| 2011 | £1,737,169 |
| 2012 | £1,220,628 |
| 2013 | £1,151,635 |
| 2014 | £2,605,965 |
| 2015 | £796,539 |
| 2016 | £760,236 |

*Source:* IFRS Annual Reports.

was due to a contribution by the Financial Accounting Foundation of £1,839,231, leaving a balance figure of £766,734.

The year 2012 was when it started to become apparent that the United States did not intend to continue with the convergence agreement, although no formal announcement was made. A reduction in contributions is a hit to IASB. In 2016 the salaries and related costs for its 137 employees amounted to £16 million, and the IASB depends on external funding. The withdrawal of the United States is a double blow. First, a major country is not using international standards, thus weakening the goal of worldwide accounting regulations. Secondly, the loss of contributions from the United States must be replaced from other sources if the IASB is to continue its work.

## The Progress of Internationalization

Although it is claimed that many countries are using international standards, it does not necessarily mean that those apply the same regulations to economic transactions. Even where a country claims it has adopted standards, caution must be present when examining the financial statements of companies within that country. The reasons are:

1. Some counties may decide to *adopt* international standards. If so, it is highly likely that the standards will apply only to certain organizations, that is, the large listed companies. Other types of organizations such as

small- and medium-sized companies will continue to rely on national standards. Some countries *adapt* international standards, in other words change them to some degree to meet their particular needs.

2. National accounting traditions are likely to continue where scope for this exists within IFRS rules. This is not to suggest that the continuation of practices is merely due to inertia, but that the reasons for the barriers to internationalization, described earlier in this chapter, remain relevant.
3. The mix of political and other pressures on regulators varies from country to country, caused partly by the financing system, legal system, and tax system. Some countries have well-organized lobby groups of finance directors. Regulators may be hesitant to fully adopt international standards because of political pressures and may delete certain paragraphs of the standards or search for part wordings where there is room for different interpretations.
4. The implementation date of a standard can vary from country to country. New standards generally are in force on the date of annual periods beginning on or after January 1, but early applications are normally permitted. The result is that two different versions of international standards can be in force at the same time depending on the implementation year chosen by a particular country compared to the choice by another country.
5. The year-ends of companies can differ. Some may find that a new international standard becomes applicable in their financial year. Others, with an earlier year-end date, will not have to comply with the IFRS until the following year's financial statements. In some countries, for example, Australia and the United Kingdom, corporate accounting periods do not necessarily end on December 31. In other countries, that may be the usual year-end date.
6. Enforcement regulations are not always stringent in some countries. Although it may be claimed that international standards have been adopted in a country, the lack of strong enforcement may mean that companies have considerable latitude in how the standards are applied.

Given all the above reasons why international accounting may not be effective, it would appear difficult to put forward an argument that international accounting works. One response is to argue that the number of countries adopting international standards has been increasing since the establishment of the IASB in 2001. This suggests that many countries do find general benefits, but there are also other specific advantages of internationalization.

1. Many small countries do not have sufficient resources to fund a rigorous standard-setting process of their own and therefore adopt international standards to ensure sound financial reporting by companies.
2. The debates generated through the process of internationalization have meant that countries have gradually changed their own practices to fit better with international standards. Although the United States has not adopted international standards, its relationship with the IASB has led to several changes to U.S. accounting practices.
3. By focusing on specific accounting issues and promoting discussions and research, the IASB has brought about a general improvement in the nature of financial accounting and reporting. This applies not only to those countries adopting international standards but to nonadopters as well.
4. A study[4] examined the effect of accounting standards and investor protection on value relevance of earnings and book value of equity among EU countries during the years 1999 to 2007. It concluded that international standards led to improvements on these issues.
5. A large sample of firms that were using international standards in 26 countries revealed that, on average, market liquidity increased around the time of the introduction of IFRS.[5] There was also a decrease in firms' cost of capital and an increase in equity valuations. Reservations on their findings included the strength of the enforcement measures in the country concerned. This is an aspect that has been observed in several studies as critical to the success of international accounting.
6. A sample[6] of non-U.S. borrowers from 40 countries during 1997 through 2005 investigated the effect of the voluntary adoption of IFRS on price and nonprice terms of loan contracts and loan ownership structure in the international loan market. It showed that

banks charge lower loan rates to IFRS adopters than to nonadopters. Banks impose more favorable nonprice terms on IFRS adopters, particularly less restrictive covenants. Banks are more willing to extend credit and IFRS adopters attract significantly more foreign lenders participating in loan syndicates than nonadopters.

## Internationalization in Individual Countries

We started this chapter by explaining the establishment of the IASC in 1973 by national accounting bodies in nine countries: Australia, Canada, France, Germany, Japan, Mexico, the Netherlands, the United Kingdom and Ireland (UK), and the United States. It is revealing to examine the progress toward international accounting by these countries, and others, at the end of 2016. There have been numerous articles written on international accounting adoption and a very useful main source of information is an excellent website that updates the position of their progress frequently.[7]

In considering the application of international standards in other countries you should remember that there are three main forces that determine general disclosure of financial and nonfinancial information by companies, as illustrated in Figure 2.2.

We would add that, in addition to the above three factors, some of the hurdles that we discussed in Chapter 1 are still present. Taxation regulations differ and the dominant culture in the country may not readily accept the principles of international accounting. The adoption of IFRSs is not merely a technical accounting decision but also a political one.

An analysis by the IFRS organization in 2017 concluded that of the 49,000 domestic listed companies on the 88 major securities exchanges

*Figure 2.2 Influences on financial disclosures*

in the world approximately some 27,000 use IFRS Standards. Of those companies not using IFRS Standards, almost 90 percent are listed in China, India, Japan, and the United States.

*Source:* http://www.ifrs.org/use-around-the-world/use-of-ifrs-standards-by-jurisdiction/#analysis.

In the following section we look at practices of those countries that attended the meeting in 1973 to agree on the development of IASs. We also examine the regulations in China, India and Japan.

### *Australia*

The Institute of Chartered Accountants first issued its Recommendations on Accounting Principles in 1946. It is argued ". . . these were virtually copies of similarly titled documents produced by the Institute of Chartered Accountants in England and Wales."[8] Possibly this similarity helped Australia to transfer to IFRSs.

The present position is that the Australian Accounting Standards Board (AASB) is the body responsible for issuing accounting standards. The AASB is an Australian government agency that develops and maintains financial reporting standards that are applicable to entities in the private and public sectors of the economy, and have the force of law for corporate entities under section 296 of the *Corporations Act 2001*. The standards must also be applied to all other general-purpose financial statements of reporting entities in the public and private sectors.

When the AASB first started to adopt IFRSs as Australian Accounting Standards, it made some modifications to the international standards. This resulted in the removal of some alternative accounting methods and adding required disclosures for the financial statements.

In 2007, the AASB modified Australian Accounting Standards so that their requirements were identical to the standards issued by the IASB for for-profit entities. Some additional disclosure requirements have been retained, and some non-IFRS-compliant requirements apply for not-for-profit and public sector entities. It is intended that compliance with Australian Accounting Standards ensures the financial statements and notes of the entity comply with IFRSs. Australia also applies the "true and fair view" concept as does the United Kingdom.

The following extract from Wesfarmers Limited Annual Report captures their legal basis:

In our opinion, the accompanying financial report of the Group is in accordance with the *Corporations Act 2001*, including:

A) giving a true and fair view of the consolidated financial position of the Group as at 30 June 2017 and of its consolidated financial performance for the year ended on that date; and
B) complying with Australian Accounting Standards and the *Corporations Regulations 2001*.

*Source:* Wesfarmers Annual Report 2017, page 140.

The costs of adopting international standards can be high for the individual companies. A survey by George, Ferguson and Spear (2012)[9] of publicly traded Australian companies concluded that there was a mean level of increased audit costs of 23 percent in the year of the transition to IFRSs. Further investigations revealed that companies with greater audit complexity, not surprisingly, experience greater increases in compliance costs for the transition to IFRSs.

### Canada

Prior to 1946, there were no accounting regulations in the country until the Canadian Institute of Chartered Accountants (CICA) commenced to issue Bulletins that codified existing practice largely as a service to their members. In 1967, the Bulletins were published in the form of an official Handbook.

There were further developments when, in 1972, the Canadian Securities Administrators issued National Policy Statement 27, requiring publicly traded companies in Canada to follow the Handbook recommendations. Three years later, the regulations implementing the Canada Business Corporations Act were revised to specify that GAAP in Canada would now be defined as the practices and guidance within the CICA Handbook.

The years from 1981 to 1998 were unusual ones in Canada. Two competing standard-setting bodies existed during this period: the CICA and the newly formed Accounting Standards Authority of Canada. It is contended that the "alternative standard-setter, the Accounting Standards Authority of Canada, experienced significant implementation issues and was unable to overcome advantages accruing to the CICA by virtue of locked-in users, first mover advantage and reputation advantage" (Richardson, 2011, 110–111).[10] It may be that some countries experience similar implementation issues if they are attempting to adopt IFRSs.

The CICA established the Accounting Standards Oversight Council (AcSOC) in 2000. The role of AcSOC is to serve the public interest by overseeing and providing input to the activities of the Accounting Standards Board (AcSB). The AcSB is responsible for establishing standards of accounting and reporting by Canadian companies and not-for-profit organizations.

The international accounting regulations developed in Canada in the early 2000s started to debate its own position. It was faced with three choices:

1. Continue to set its own standards. This would be an expensive activity and separate it from the practices of many other countries.
2. Adopt U.S. standards. This would be inexpensive but may make it appear as merely a follower of its more powerful neighbor.
3. Adopt international standards. This would be expensive but would demonstrate its position as a player in the global business market. There was also the fact that the United States had started its convergence project and would, most likely, converge fully with IFRSs at a future date.

Given these scenarios, in January of 2006, the AcSB published a strategic plan to implement IFRSs. These have been mandatory in Canada since 2011 for Publicly Accountable Entities. The application of IFRSs in Canada, therefore, is broader than in Europe as it applies to many more types of entities.

Publicly Accountable Entities are profit-orientated enterprises that have responsibilities to a large or diverse group of stakeholders and include:

- Publicly listed companies
- Enterprises with fiduciary responsibilities, such as banks, insurance companies, credit unions, securities firms, mutual funds, and investment banks
- Certain government corporations

Several Canadian companies have been listed on U.S. stock exchanges for many years. The current Canadian regulations provide an option for those companies to apply U.S. GAAP rather than Canadian GAAP.

There are entities in Canada, and some other countries, known as rate-regulated companies. These have a monopoly or dominant market position and provide goods and services such as electricity, gas, telephone service, water, and television cable to the general public. Regulatory bodies or governments are those that determine the prices that can be charged to customers for the services or products. Such entities had technical difficulties in complying with IFRSs. The issue of IFRS 14 Regulatory Deferred Accounts resolved the issues and compliance with IFRSs commenced for annual periods beginning on or after January 1, 2015.

As with Australia, the evidence of compliance with IFRSs can be found in the Auditors Report. The following extract is taken from a large Canadian company.

> In our opinion, the consolidated financial statements present fairly, in all material respects, the financial position of Empire Company Limited as at May 7, 2016 and its financial performance and its cash flows for the 53-week period then ended in accordance with International Financial Reporting Standards.
>
> *Source:* Empire Annual Report 2016, page 66.

Experiences in Canada support the findings on costs of adoption in Australia. A survey by the Canadian Financial Executives Research Foundation[11] (2013) examined the transition costs and the recurring costs. The average total transition cost for larger-sized companies was $4,041,177. The lowest amount spent by a large company was $80,000 and the highest cost was $25.5 million. A perspective on the significance of the cost is given by comparing it to revenue. Costs as a percentage of revenues were 0.006 percent for the lowest spender and 0.08 percent for the highest spender.

As far as recurring costs are concerned, these can be separated into those for preparing the annual report and accounts and those for the interim financial statements. For the annual report and accounts, 48 percent of respondents reported that their costs were about the same. Fifteen percent reported cost savings. These arose from not having to reconcile their financial statements with U.S. GAAP, reducing the number of accounting frameworks the organization had to apply. The remainder (37 percent) reported that complying with IFRS proved to be more costly.

### *The European Union*

All domestic companies in the European Union whose securities are traded in a public market are required to use IFRS Standards as adopted by the European Union in their consolidated financial statements. Traded in a public market refers to a stock exchange. The EU Accounting Regime requires that each IFRS is adopted individually for use in the European Union. The adoption process is sometimes referred to as "endorsement." The process is as follows:

- The IASB issues a standard or an amendment to a standard.
- EFRAG (the European Financial Reporting Advisory Group) holds consultations with interest groups. EFRAG is an important and essential part of the adoption process.
- EFRAG delivers its advice to the European Commission whether the standard meets the criteria of endorsement. It also conducts an effect study about the potential economic effects of the given standard's application in the European Union.

Based on the advice of EFRAG, the Commission prepares a draft endorsement Regulation. The European Accounting Regulatory Committee (ARC), set up in accordance with Article 6 of the IAS Regulation, votes on the Commission proposal. If the vote is favorable the European

Parliament and the Council of the European Union have 3 months to oppose the adoption of the draft Regulation by the Commission.

If the European Parliament and the Council give their favorable opinion on the adoption and 3 months elapsed without opposition from their side, the Commission adopts the draft Regulation. After adoption, it is published in the *Official Journal* and enters into force on the day laid down in the Regulation itself.

In assessing whether a particular IFRS should be adopted in the European Union, the Regulation requires that it:

- be consistent with the true and fair view,
- be conducive to the public good in Europe and,
- meet basic criteria on the quality of information required for financial statements to satisfy users' needs.

The time to review and adopt a new standard is lengthy. However, the only difference between IFRS and EU-adopted IFRS has been a "carve-out" of a few sentences in IAS 39 that barred the use of a form of hedge accounting applied by a minority of European banks.

The following example of an Independent Auditor's Report is extracted from the Annual Report and Accounts of the UK Burberry Group plc.:

In our opinion, Burberry Group plc's Group financial statements (the "financial statements"):

- give a true and fair view of the state of the Group's affairs as at 31 March 2017 and of its profit and cash flows for the year then ended;
- have been properly prepared in accordance with International Financial Reporting Standards ("IFRSs") as adopted by the European Union; and
- have been prepared in accordance with the requirements of the Companies Act 2006 and Article 4 of the IAS Regulation.

*Source: Burberry Group plc Annual Report, 2016/7, page 119.*

There are several items that are noteworthy and emphasize the difference between UK accounting and U.S. accounting. These are:

- For UK companies, financial statements must give a true and fair view. This is not a concept shared by the United States and many other countries.

- The statements have been prepared in accordance with IFRSs **as adopted by the European Union**. It is unusual for the EU not to adopt IFRSs fully, but one must be aware that possibility exists.
- The statements have also been prepared in accordance with the UK Companies Act 2006. Other EU companies have their own national legislation as illustrated in the following example from a French-based company:

The Statutory Auditors' report includes information specifically required by French law in such reports, whether modified or not. This information is presented below the audit opinion on the Consolidated Financial Statements and includes an explanatory paragraph discussing the Auditors' assessments of certain significant accounting and auditing matters. These assessments were considered for the purpose of issuing an audit opinion on the Consolidated Financial Statements taken as a whole and not to provide separate assurance on individual account balances, transactions, or disclosures.

To the Shareholders,

In compliance with the assignment entrusted to us by your shareholders' meetings, we hereby report to you, for the year ended December 31, 2016, on:

- the audit of the accompanying Consolidated Financial Statements of Carrefour "the Group";
- the justification of our assessments;
- the specific verification required by French law.

The Consolidated Financial Statements have been approved by the Board of Directors. Our role is to express an opinion on these Consolidated Financial Statements based on our audit.

*Source:* Carrefour Group Annual Report and Accounts 2016, pages 245–6.

We emphasize that the company, as a member of the European Union, complies with international standards. However, as with other countries that are members of the European Union, there are national legal requirements that also require compliance. Explanation of these is outside the focus of this book and, when examining the financial statements of EU companies, you can assume that they comply fully with international standards. You must also be aware that national legislation may also affect some disclosures.

The current position is with Britain being a member of the European Union. We are now confronted with "Brexit" and the declared intention of Britain withdrawing from the European Union. At this stage it is uncertain how this will affect international accounting, bearing in mind that the offices of the IASB are in London, England. The Institute of Chartered Accountants in England and Wales has identified several possible courses of action[12]:

1. IFRS adopted by the EU procedure would be applied by UK listed companies.

   This would be a simple and inexpensive route but it does mean that the United Kingdom has ceded authority to the EU process. This could mean that the United Kingdom would be required to comply with standards with which it did not agree.
2. UK companies comply with standards issued by the IASB and ignore EU procedures.

   This could mean that UK companies must comply with standards with which the United Kingdom does not agree and has had no opportunity to be a party to the decision making.
3. A UK process that decided whether a standard should be endorsed.

   This option is an expensive choice but has advantages. The process of adoption would be a powerful influence on the IASBs' decision making as it would not wish to issue a standard that a major country rejected. It also ensures that UK listed companies must comply with a standard that recognizes the particular concerns and conditions in the United Kingdom.

In its publication the ICAEW proposes that the third option is the most preferable. Its discussions with others have shown that there is conditional support for this option. The argument in its favor is that most developed economies that have adopted IFRS have had some form of national endorsement mechanism. Also, the experience with EU endorsement shows that there have been few decisions that have disrupted the process.

There are some possible drawbacks. Decisions made by the United Kingdom may not correspond with those made in the EU endorsement process. This could lead to the United Kingdom and the European Union having different versions of an IFRS. Until the law and regulations post-Brexit are resolved it is impossible to determine how these issues can be resolved.

In the academic literature there have been several articles concerning the meaning of the word "adoption." Zeff and Nobes (2010)[13] claim that adoption means the full-scale voluntary use by a company of IFRSs as issued by the IASB, before such use became compulsory in its jurisdiction. Some would regard this as a very narrow definition but in their examination of several companies they concluded that:

1. Not all of the IFRS content is always included in the national version;
2. Not all companies in a country are compelled to use IFRSs;
3. In some countries companies can voluntarily use IFRSs;
4. Company financial reports do not always contain a statement that they do comply with IFRSs.

The authors offer suggestions to improve the full compliance with IFRSs, but the reality may be that countries want full control of the financial information provided by companies. The IASB can issue accounting standards but it has no authority to compel countries or companies to completely comply with them. Understandably, countries wish to retain control of the companies operating in its borders and, although financial information is important, countries require companies to also make public other information including corporate governance. We discuss these developments in the final chapter.

### *Mexico*

This country was a member of the group of country representatives that met in 1973 to discuss the internationalization of accounting regulations. On November 11, 2008, the Mexican SEC (Comisión Nacional Bancaria y de Valores [CNBV]) announced that all companies listed on the Mexican Stock Exchange would be required to comply with IFRS starting in 2012. Listed companies would have the option to comply with IFRS earlier—starting as early as 2008—subject to requirements that would be established by the CNBV.

In the period 2008 to 2010, the Mexican Institute of Certified Public Accountants auditing commission issued some amended auditing regulations to correspond with the international standards' requirements. Additionally, IFRSs were translated into the local language. This assisted in the adoption of the standards. In 2012, domestically listed companies, except for financial institutions, commenced to use IFRSs as was the government intention.

Interestingly, Steinback and Tan (2014)[14] have found that the adoption of IFRS has led Mexican companies to change some of their business practices. Two examples they provide are behavioral and strategic changes in areas such as hedging strategy. With such transactions the complexity of the IFRS standard has reduced hedging strategy and sales because contractual terms have to be amended to comply with IFRS. The article also includes the example of Coca-Cola FEMSA, which changed from Mexican GAAP to IFRSs. The company identified where there are optional accounting treatments, compared with the practices of foreign companies using IFRSs, prepared a formal strategy, and implemented a training program.

### *China*

China was differently placed than the market-based economies that had adopted international standards. It had state ownership of many companies, underdeveloped capital markets, and a lack of qualified accountants.[15] The country, therefore, chose the path of convergence rather than full adoption. In 2006, the IASB stated that Chinese standards were substantially converged with IFRS Standards. In addition, China has committed to adopt IFRS Standards for reporting by at least some domestic companies. The IASB also noted that several Chinese companies already produced IFRS-compliant financial statements because of their dual listings in Hong Kong and other international markets.

The movement to the adoption of international standards has led to other significant changes. One study[16] found that the impact of IFRS convergence led to a decrease in conservatism used by companies but this was limited to geographic areas with high institutional quality. One effect of IFRS adoption was a growth in executive compensation as IFRS adoption led to a reduction in accounting conservatism, which was a feature of the previous regulations.

At this stage, it is impossible to predict whether full convergence will take place. One can argue that, although China is different from many other countries, it is now taking a global position and there may be a trend toward a market-based economy. One study[17] found that nonstate-owned enterprises viewed the change more favorably, especially those with a greater need for external financing. Their research demonstrated that the convergence toward IFRS in China has significant consequences for investors (i.e., in terms of value relevance). It is not merely a political decision in response to the thrust of international accounting harmonization.

There would appear to be several barriers to China seeking further convergence. In particular, it remains a basic Confusion culture and finds a rules-based approach more acceptable than the IASBs principles-based approach. In addition, state-owned enterprises still dominate the economy and the restrictions on foreign investors reduce their demand.

There are few indications that there will be a move to full adoption of all IASs. There are also no obvious forces that would encourage China to make further efforts toward full convergence. Although this may be a disappointment for enthusiasts, the evidence suggests that there are boundaries to convergence.

### *India*

India has Indian Accounting Standards (Ind-AS) that had been developed by the Institute of Chartered Accountants of India (ICAI). The Securities and Exchange Board of India (SEBI) had the legal authority to require all listed companies with subsidiaries to file consolidated financial statements complying with these standards. There was also an option for listed companies to opt to comply with international standards but only a very small number did so.

It is claimed[18] that India has been in a state of gradual convergence with IFRS since 2007. In 2013, India revised its Companies Act to require listed and large companies to prepare consolidated financial statements in conformity with a new set of Ind-AS to be adopted by the ICAI. In 2015, the Ministry of Corporate Affairs announced its road map for adopting Ind-AS for 2016–2017. There is no complete convergence and differences remain in accounting for business combinations, control, financial instruments, and revenues.

The extent to which the convergence route will go is uncertain. Companies must comply with Ind-AS and these standards are based on IFRSs. However, there appears to be support offered by the Ind-IAS, although there were significant reservations on the awareness and challenges in the preparation for IFRS-based standards.

### *Japan*

IFRS Standards are one of four permitted financial reporting frameworks for domestic listed companies. The others are Japanese GAAP, Japan's Modified International Standards, and U.S. GAAP. The various studies that have been conducted suggest that there is considerable resistance to the full adoption of international standards.

One study[19] considered the barriers to full adoption and identified a series of different environments that would prove problematic. One is the societal environment that is influenced by Confucianism. There is a work culture based on loyalty and the avoidance of conflict and values of thrift and moderation. Any new practices tend to be integrated into existing practices instead of replacing them.

The organizational environment has a large number of publicly traded listed companies but 99 percent of Japanese companies are privately owned and small in size. Companies tend to progress by making long-term relationships and avoiding competition and there are only a relatively small number of professionally qualified accountants.

The process of introducing internationalization comes under the authority of the Financial Services Agency. The authors comment that there could well be differences between "IFRS as issued by the IASB" and those "endorsed by the FSA."

The difficulty of combining the aim of converging with the reality of the existing framework and international practices is illustrated in a study by Noriyuki Tsunogaya.[20] A content analysis of relevant meetings of the Business Accounting Council of Japan was conducted. The authors concluded that it would be difficult to adopt fully international standards because of the need to achieve international comparability and maintain institutional complementarity between financial reporting and infrastructures such as accounting-relating laws.

A similar picture is also demonstrated in a study of Japanese financial executives.[21] Although there is considerable discussion on convergence the authors conclude that the situation is similar to that of the United States. The AcSB of Japan is created to promote convergence with international standards being introduced in 2016, but that aim has been delayed indefinitely.

The authors conducted a survey with senior financial executives of 292 Japanese listed companies in 2013 to 2014. On the basis of their findings they concluded that a significant percentage of respondents consider the costs of IFRS to be a major impact but the benefits would be only moderate. Those perceiving substantial benefits were the large and overseas companies. As we mentioned earlier, the majority of Japanese companies are small and privately owned.

## Limits of Internationalization

There is a danger in seeing the adoption of international accounting by a country as the only alternative to its use of its own national accounting. The encouragement for countries to adopt international accounting suggests that it is always the best method for all countries and the companies within their boundaries. The evidence suggests that this is not necessarily always the case and barriers to full convergence remain.

There are some advantages in adopting international standards. The time and expense for a small country to develop its own standards can be considerable. Although the adoption of international standards may require a levy to the IASB, it is usually less expensive than home-developed standards. The advantages for international companies or those companies connected in some way with international organizations are beneficial. All speak the same international language of finance.

However, smaller, national companies and their business contacts may be perfectly satisfied with their own national regulations. Being compelled to comply with the complexities of national standards can be very expensive. The IASB is aware of this problem and has issued the *IFRS for SMEs* Standard. This is approximately 250 pages and is intended for smaller companies. The users of such financial statements are identified by the IASB as lenders, creditors, and other users of SME financial statements. The emphasis of the information is directed at the disclosure of information on cash flows, liquidity, and solvency.

There are disadvantages of full adoption of international standards, which are rarely discussed. Possibly the most important is that countries have their own legislation to control business activities. They would not wish to relinquish part of their authority unless there were persuasive arguments to do so. There are also cultural and business practices that are fundamental to the country and we demonstrated these in our earlier discussions in this chapter. Finally, there is a large expense incurred. Companies may have to change their methods for collecting and recording data, auditors will need to become proficient in the new requirements, investors and other users may have to improve their capabilities, and accounting lecturers may have to change all their teaching notes.

## Conclusion

The defects and problems of national accounting regulations are easy to understand. Imagine that you are in the United States and wish to buy goods from a company in Germany. You do a financial investigation and find that they appear to be a well-established company that made a healthy profit last year.

You discuss this with an accounting friend who examines the German company's accounts and declares that the company had, in fact, made a loss. You are confused but even more so when your friend explains that different countries use different methods to measure company performance. You want to know whether there is a profit or loss. Being told it depends on how you do your calculations does not help.

Looking from a different viewpoint, you may be a company seeking additional finance for expansion of your business. You may be at the stage to list on a stock exchange. If you are in a country that already has IFRSs, you could list on its stock exchange. If it retains its own standard setting, you may have to draw up your financial statements using those national regulations.

The arguments for international accounting are compelling, although the barriers have, historically, been difficult to surmount. However, over recent years, they have been eroded gradually. International accounting has become more widespread, although its application in particular countries is not as rigorous as it could be. The IASB has no authority to monitor what companies are doing or enforce compliance so the full effect of international accounting is not fully known.

The research indicates that there are benefits to be enjoyed from adopting IFRS set by the IASB. The countries that make up the European Union have followed the route of complete adoption and it has been successful. There is also the path of convergence, in other words a country issuing their own standards based on the requirements of the IFRS. But for some countries which we have used as examples in this chapter, full convergence is difficult to achieve and may not even be desired.

There is also the contentious question as to what is meant by adoption of international standards. The research available shows that many countries go through a convergence process but do not fully adopt all IASs. Also, all companies in that country are not obliged to comply with international standards and usually it is only companies listed on a stock exchange. The evidence shows that we do not have full adoption on a global basis of international standards. The United States provides the main example of a country that commenced on the route of convergence, followed it for several years, and then withdrew. In the following chapter, we will discuss U.S. involvement in international accounting and how we have arrived at the present U.S. position.

# CHAPTER 3

# The Convergence Project

## About This Chapter

The United States had been a supporter of international accounting since 1973 and was a very active participant for the period from 2002 to 2012. It directed considerable resources into the development of International Financial Reporting Standards (IFRS) issued by the International Accounting Standards Board (IASB) and, at the same time, changed parts of its own regulations so that they complemented the international approach to accounting issues.

Unlike other jurisdictions, including Australia, Canada, and countries in the European Union (EU), the Financial Accounting Standards Board (FASB) chose not to adopt IFRS as originally drafted. Instead, it worked with the IASB in developing standards that both Boards found acceptable. By choosing this convergence approach, U.S. accounting regulations have been heavily influenced by international thinking and alterations have been made to existing U.S. regulations.

Many believed, or at least hoped, that the convergence approach would finally lead to the United States fully adopting IFRS. Despite comments from the FASB and several road maps showing the route it intended to take, the United States has withdrawn from the convergence project and decided to follow its own path.

In this chapter, we explain the route that the United States has selected with regard to international accounting standards (IASs), and the debate on internationalization that has taken place within the country. We complete the chapter by considering two underlying issues that have not been resolved: the definition of high-quality standards and the conflict between a principles-based approach and a rules-based approach in setting accounting standards.

## The Early Commitment

The lengthy and arduous progress of the relationship between the United States and international standard setters has been extremely well described by Kirsch.[1] The study incorporates not only documentary evidence, but also correspondence with some of the major decision makers. This section draws from that work and also adds material from other relevant sources.

In the first few years following the International Accounting Standards Committee's (IASC) formation in 1973, there was limited contact between the Committee and the FASB. The IASC was, however, gradually spreading its influence with an increasing number of smaller countries deciding to follow international standards. It was not until 1988, when the IASC had issued nearly 30 separate standards, that the FASB publicly announced its position on international accounting. It stated that the Board would support the development of superior international standards that would then gradually supplant national standards as the superior standards became universally accepted.

There were issues, however, that could prevent, or at least delay, such an occurrence. One of these, which was not discussed at that time, was how international standards could be identified as "superior." We return to this topic when we consider the development of "high-quality" standards. The issues that could cause immediate problems were:

1. The differing national objectives of financial reporting.
2. The wide spectrum of national standard-setting structures from predominantly government-led to predominantly private-sector standards.
3. Nationalism and the reluctance to relinquish control to an outside body.
4. The particular economic, political, and social priorities of different nations.

Notwithstanding the challenges, the FASB believed that it could contribute to improving international standards in many ways. It clearly demonstrated its enthusiasm for international standards by declaring that it would take the following steps:

1. Join the IASC Consultative Group.
2. Expand and strengthen relationships with national standard-setting bodies.

3. Greater systematic analysis of international accounting literature relating to major FASB projects.
4. Encourage more comments on FASB Exposure Drafts from an international perspective.
5. Hold discussions with IASC leadership on holding an international conference of national standard setters on accounting conceptual frameworks.
6. Recruit accountants with foreign experience to join the FASB staff.

In 1991, the FASB published an authoritative article[2] on its plans for international activities, which was based on two key assumptions. The first assumption was that domestic financial reporting needs would continue to be the FASB's first priority. The second assumption was that its international activities would be conducted within its charter and mission statement. These assumptions would seem to limit considerably the FASB from adopting international standards. In retrospect, one may conclude that there was not an overwhelming desire to move toward convergence, but rather a wish to be involved.

The declaration by the FASB for greater international involvement was met with enthusiasm by the IASC. It was difficult to claim that IFRSs were international when the largest market did not adopt them. In addition, some countries, without their own national Generally Accepted Accounting Principles (GAAP), followed U.S. GAAP. The move by the FASB toward international accounting would encourage these countries to follow the same route.

In 1996, the SEC indicated that it supported the IASC's objective to develop accounting standards that could be accepted when preparing the necessary financial statements in cross-border offerings. The elements of the IASC's strategy were a core set of comprehensive, generally accepted accounting pronouncements, which were of high quality and resulted in three elements: comparability, transparency, and full disclosure for users. These standards were expected to be rigorously interpreted and applied.

If the IASC achieved these three elements, it was the SEC's intention to consider permitting foreign issuers offering securities in the United States to draw up their financial statements by applying international standards. It would be some 10 years before this consideration became a reality.

Both the SEC and FASB had expressed their support for international accounting. In the year 1999, the FASB[3] and its oversight body, the Financial Accounting Foundation, issued a report making public their vision for the future of international accounting. They regarded the desired outcome as the worldwide use of a single set of high-quality accounting standards for both domestic and cross-border financial reporting. To achieve that, the FASB would be required to:

- Take a leadership role in the evolution of international accounting.
- Commit to the required resources to ensure that international standards were of a high quality.

It was accepted that, if a quality IAS setting structure and process were established, it could lead to structural and procedural changes to the FASB, as well as potential changes in its national role. It would no longer be the rule setter in the United States. It is not clear whether various parties in the United States fully recognized the implications that the control of standard setting would be held by the IASC.

It would appear that the United States regarded itself as first among equals. In pursuing this vision of international regulations, the FASB stated that it should retain its worldwide leadership role in standard setting and believed that "Worldwide acceptance of internationally recognized standards and a global standard-setting process is impossible without U.S. acceptance and participation" (FASB 1999, 1).[3]

The intentions of the United States were welcomed by the IASC. Although it had made considerable progress, prior to the year 2000, the major national economies, including Australia, Canada, the United Kingdom, and the United States, were still complying with their own national accounting standards. These national standards frequently differed significantly from international standards. If international accounting was to become a reality, either a complete overhaul of all aspects of the IASC was required, or a new and more powerful body needed to be formed. The latter was the course of action chosen.

The IASB was established formally in April 2001 with the objectives of:

- Developing in the public interest a single set of high-quality, understandable, and enforceable global accounting standards;
- Helping participants in the world's capital markets and other users make economic decisions by having access to high-quality, transparent, and comparable information;
- Promoting the use and vigorous application of those standards;
- Bringing about convergence of national accounting standards and IASs to produce high-quality solutions to accounting issues faced by companies across the globe.

In 2002, the recently appointed chair of the IASB, David Tweedie, made clear his aim of spreading IASs to the United States. He declared that the IASB's two main objectives were:

1. *Convergence of U.S. and international standards.* Possibly, Tweedie realized that it was unrealistic to expect the United States to adopt existing IFRSs in one sweep. The most feasible route was to converge IFRSs and U.S. GAAP. Convergence in this context is defined as jointly agreeing on changes to both sets of standards to produce one set of high-quality, global accounting regulations.
2. *An improvement project.* This was seen as the first step to promote convergence on high-quality standards. The Board's objective was to revise and reissue 12 named IASC standards by the first half of 2003.

The appointment in July 2002 of a new FASB chair, Robert Herz, added a fresh international dimension to the United States' way of thinking. Herz was a qualified UK Chartered Accountant and had previously served on the IASB. His appointment brought with it a greater commitment to convergence, which complemented the objectives of the restructured IASB under David Tweedie. The rapport led to the signing in 2002 of the Norwalk Agreement, which had the objective of converging U.S. standards and international standards.

The position adopted by the IASB was formed at a time when both internal and external factors strengthened the argument for convergence. The New York Stock Exchange (NYSE) was facing growing competition from markets in other countries, while foreign companies were finding that the U.S. requirements, such as the Sarbanes–Oxley Act, were becoming increasingly onerous. In addition, a succession of financial scandals such as Enron and WorldCom weakened confidence in U.S. financial reporting regulations and the effectiveness of the rules-based approach to regulation.

External pressures were also becoming apparent. First, several countries had either adopted international accounting or were planning to do so, which meant that the United States could potentially lose its vision of becoming a world leader. It would not be leading the international standard setting and could become isolated. Secondly, the IASB was proving a much more effective organization than the IASC and was generating support from many organizations while simultaneously improving its standards. Finally, new capital markets that already recognized international standards were expanding abroad and threatening New York's claim as the premier capital market.

## The Norwalk Agreement

As a consequence of the pressures generated by the above events, it is not surprising that in October 2002, the FASB and the newly formed IASB signed an agreement in Norwalk, Connecticut. This agreement sets out the aims of the two Boards and the actions they intended to take jointly.

### *Aims*

- The existing financial reporting standards of the FASB and the IASB would become fully compatible as soon as practicable.
- The future work programs of the two bodies would be coordinated to ensure that once compatibility was achieved, compatibility of standards would be maintained.

### *Priority Actions*

- To undertake a short-term project aimed at removing a variety of individual differences between U.S. GAAP and IFRS.

- To remove other differences between IFRS and U.S. GAAP that remained on January 1, 2005, through coordination of future work programs. This would require the Boards to invest the time and resources to undertake substantial projects.
- To continue progress on the joint projects that were currently being undertaken.
- To encourage their respective interpretative bodies to coordinate their activities.

The problems faced by the two parties in following the convergence route chosen were probably underestimated. With some confidence it was claimed that the differences between U.S. GAAP and internationalization were not insurmountable.[4] However, a few years later it was recognized that "for many countries convergence with international accounting standards will be a monumental task."[5] Not surprisingly, although "the goal of their convergence efforts was common standards, they sometimes fell short of that objective" (Kirsch 2012, 47).[6]

There was also the issue that seems to be overlooked, which is that convergence would involve changes to existing international standards. This meant that all those countries that had already adopted them would have to make amendments to their accounting practices. The users of the financial statements would need to become accustomed to the new requirements and the preparers would need to change their procedures to collect the required data, and, finally, the auditors would need to be thoroughly familiar with the new requirements.

Any changes to accounting standards are extremely disruptive and expensive. A learning process has to take place with accountants, auditors, and the users of financial statements. It also means that it is extremely difficult to compare this year's financial results with those of previous years. Is the difference in the profit trend due to changes in accounting or the performance of the company? For all parties this represents challenges. The convergence project partnered by the FASB and the IASB offered stability and high-quality standards.

## The Challenges

When assessing the extent of adoption by countries, care must be taken in making assumptions on what this action means in a particular country.

Some jurisdictions will adopt IASs completely. Some may not adopt them fully but adapt them by passing the standards through their own regulatory procedures. The adopted standards may therefore be modified to some extent to correspond with perceived national needs and existing practices. Finally, some countries will issue standards that they claim are similar to, or based on, IFRS, which implies that there still remain differences. It is therefore difficult to state categorically how many countries are using IASs in their complete and original form. It is even more difficult to know the extent to which individual companies comply with the standards and the enforcement procedures in place in a particular country.

Where a country claims to be following international standards, it does not follow that all types and sizes of companies in that country are complying with them. Normally, companies listed on the country's stock exchange will be expected to apply international standards, although some banks and other financial institutions may be exempt. Smaller, private companies with less complex operations and fewer resources will not be applying full international standards. They may be following a simplified version or the country may have issued its own accounting standards for smaller entities. The IASB issued in 2009 *FRS for Small and Medium-Sized Entities.*

Another key factor in the internationalization debate is the strength of enforcement practices in a particular country. The IASB only issues standards; it does not conduct any surveillance to ascertain whether the standards are strictly followed. National regulators and auditors have the responsibility of ensuring that regulations are followed, and the effectiveness of their actions may not always be very high.

Finally, corporate financial reporting not only reflects the requirements and enforcement of accounting standards, but it is argued that influences such as legal institutions, capital market forces, product market competition, and governance are also involved in shaping the financial disclosures made by companies.[7]

A further concern regarding internationalization is that the standard-setting process involves a compromise among a large and very diverse set of constituents from around the world. Countries have differing objectives with respect to financial reporting regulations. Although the United States has the objective that financial reporting satisfies the needs of external investors, companies in other countries may rely heavily on close relationships among a large set of stakeholders for financing, and are less focused on capital markets.

Given the practices in other countries, the IASB had to attempt to modify or develop IFRSs to meet the demands of insider or stakeholder economies. Thus, IFRS may not be able to satisfy the objectives of U.S. financial reporting, which is to meet the needs of investors and others directly involved with financial reporting.

The following section concentrates, therefore, on the attitudes and opinions within the United States. In that country there are many interest groups with differing opinions on involvement in the development of international standards. The views within each of these groups can change as time passes and new events occur. The following sections examine the opinions of five interested groups. They capture the main thrust of their opinions, but also attempt to reflect differences and changes through time.

## Opinions on U.S. Internationalization

### *Regulatory Bodies*

The United States has been setting accounting standards for over half a century. This has involved a substantial investment and has resulted in a highly sophisticated system of accounting regulation. Abandoning completely the success that has been achieved does not appear to be an attractive proposition.

A positive argument for U.S. regulators to recognize and adopt international standards is that there is a potentially wider political benefit for the United States. A strong message is made public that U.S. regulators wish to cooperate with other major countries on important global business issues. It reinforces the reputation of the United States as a global force.

Although it may be impossible for the FASB to adopt fully IASs, the Board's involvement ensures that the United States is in a position to greatly influence the development of standards. Given the size of its international trade and capital markets, it can make a valuable contribution to the improvement of international standards.

At the other end of the spectrum, there are potentially negative consequences if the United States does not adopt fully international standards or play a major role in their formation. As international standards become more widely established, multinational corporations may find that they meet their strategies and policies. It is even possible that U.S standards could become an ineffective competitor relative to an increasingly dominant international body.

There are also more specific reasons for some form of U.S. involvement. One reason put forward is that regulators have seen a significant shift in global market capitalization, with U.S. market share steadily declining.[8] There are various influences that operate over time to determine the market share of a particular stock exchange, although the data does suggest some erosion in the popularity of the U.S. market.

The NYSE market cap at the end of 2003 was 41 times that of the Bombay Stock Exchange (BSE) and 31 times that of Shanghai Exchange. In July 2009, the NYSE was 9 times that of BSE and only 3.6 times that of Shanghai.[9]

According to the September 2009 Standard & Poor report, the U.S. market was less than 41 percent of global capital markets, a substantial decline from January 2004, when it was nearly 53 percent.[10]

This decline in U.S. market share must be considered in the context of other events, in particular the state of the economy. In the first few months of 2014, 42 Initial Public Offerings (IPOs) were listed on the NYSE or NASDAQ. In the last 12 months, there have been many more IPOs listing on the NYSE and NASDAQ than in any other country. The Global Financial Centre Index shows that in 2014 London had lost the top spot it has had for 7 years and was in second place behind New York.[11] However, there are always changes and, in 2017, it was declared that London, New York, Singapore, Hong Kong, and Tokyo were the top five financial centers in that order.

There are still arguments for regulators to remain involved and continue to participate in international standard setting, but there is also an opposing view. It is claimed that the political incentives that fostered convergence efforts between the United States and the IASB were mostly short term, and there are no evident incentives for U.S. firms to adopt international standards.

There is also a well-documented history of American exceptionalism as a means of defending U.S. sovereignty in matters of U.S. foreign policy. This stance is not particular to the United States and most countries wish to retain authority over the regulations applied in their own country.

Although the United States has now abandoned the convergence project, it is possible that it may decide to, once again, attempt full internationalization. If so, there is the question whether the SEC has the legal authority to delegate its regulatory powers regarding financial reporting by U.S. companies to a foreign, private body of standard setters.[12]

### *U.S. Corporates*

Corporates, when taking a position on the adoption of IFRS, will be attempting to weigh the benefits against the costs of changing their accounting systems. Undoubtedly, there are costs and benefits if all corporates are using the same accounting system. The following factors may persuade some corporates that an IFRS reporting has its benefits[13]:

- Some U.S. companies already report using IFRS because it is the subsidiary of an international parent or has an investor company, and these demand IFRS reporting.
- If the U.S. company has foreign subsidiaries that are required to follow IFRS reporting in their own countries, it is simpler and cheaper for the entire group to follow IFRS.
- Where there are operations in other countries, those jurisdictions may make IFRS reporting mandatory.
- Although U.S. companies are required to follow U.S. GAAP reporting, they may choose to disclose statements with IFRS-based reports to allow for an accurate comparison with foreign competitors.

As always, there are cost–benefit calculations to be taken into account. The costs of transferring from U.S. regulations to IFRS can be high and can include the following:

- Existing accounting staff will require training and additional staff with experience will have to be recruited;

- Information systems will require substantial changes;
- Multiple charts of accounts and consolidation methods will need to be coordinated;
- Standardization of policies and procedures needs to be implemented for consistency in standards in different jurisdictions;
- Company's strategies may need to be reviewed as new financial information becomes available;
- Management information systems need to be reviewed;
- Managers will need to be trained to understand the information available and its implications on planning, control, and decision-making responsibilities.

There are always problems in making cost comparisons based on other countries' experiences, but the transition to IFRS by Canada gives some insights. For larger-sized companies, defined as organizations with revenues of CDN$1 billion or more, the average total cost of transitioning was CDN$4,041,177. The lowest spent by a large company was CDN$80,000, by a financial services company with revenues of more than CDN$1.28 billion. The highest cost in the category was CDN$25.5 million, spent by a financial services company with revenues of CDN$30 billion. Costs as a percentage of revenues were 0.006 percent for the lowest spender and 0.08 percent for the highest spender in the category.[14]

### *Foreign Listers*

Foreign companies that wish to list in the United States now have three options regarding their mandatory SEC filings. They can provide reports under IASs as issued by the IASB, use U.S. GAAP, or file reports in their own domestic GAAP with reconciliation to U.S. GAAP. Clearly, if a foreign company is required by the regulations in its own country to comply with IFRS, the first option appears the most sensible.

One study investigated the decisions made by foreign companies confronting these options.[15] It found an increase of 20 percent (30 firms) in the group of IFRS-reporting firms over the two-year sample period, whereas the fraction of foreign filers that use U.S. GAAP or domestic accounting standards decreased by 4 percent (12 firms) and 7 percent

(18 firms), respectively. In addition, the total number of foreign filers from countries requiring the use of IASs increased from 137 firms in 2009 to 173 firms in 2010 (26 percent). Within this group, there was an increase of international reporting by 35 firms.

Given the growth of international reporting in the world and the elimination of the reconciliation requirements in the United States, it may have been assumed that there would be more cross-listed companies filing IFRS reports with the SEC. There are two reasons that this may not have happened.

First, foreign cross-listed firms from countries that have not adopted international standards may have been listed in the United States for some years. Their original choice of accounting standards would have been U.S. GAAP or domestic GAAP with reconciliation to U.S. GAAP. There would be costs associated with the change to international standards. Furthermore, the users of their financial statements are most likely more familiar with U.S. GAAP.

Another reason for not using IFRS for filing may be that the companies consider that U.S. GAAP is of higher quality, and that the rules-based approach in the United States provides clearer guidance and direction on what to report and how. The AAA FRPC[16] argues that although both IFRS and U.S. GAAP represent a high-quality set of accounting standards, it is less certain whether IFRS provides equivalent financial reporting quality relative to U.S. GAAP. In a survey of U.S. accounting professors, only 13 percent of the respondents considered IFRS to be of better quality than U.S. GAAP.[17]

Finally, U.S. GAAP has been a dominant system for many years. Foreign companies and foreign investors know the regulations and have confidence in them. The possible incentives to change to IFRS may not be sufficient for that change to take place.

### *Investors*

The key benefit claimed for international accounting is the comparability of financial information. Individuals, groups, and corporates conduct their investments in an ever-increasingly integrated world of capital markets. In such a world, there is a need for comparability and transparency of financial reporting worldwide to allow for easy comparison of the financial results of a manufacturing company in, for example, France with those in the United States, Australia, and anywhere else in the world.

Of course, U.S. investors also operate in jurisdictions where international standards are the required standards for financial reporting. A study examined whether mandatory IAS adoption at the national level lowers U.S. investors' tendency to overweigh domestic stocks in their common stock portfolios.[18] The results showed that a common set of global accounting standards is helpful for portfolio holdings of U.S. investors. Interestingly, they also observed that the enforcement of standards in a country is a crucial determinant when making investments outside the United States.

It would seem that from the investors' viewpoint, a global set of accounting standards is preferable. However, this does depend on the quality of those standards and the levels of compliance and enforcement in a particular country.

### *Accounting Profession*

There can be financial benefits in changing regulations for those who provide services, but it can be a two-edged sword. Where a company has to move from U.S. GAAP to international regulations, accounting advice, at a cost, will be required. However, if accountants are offering their services to companies with international connections, they receive fees from constructing financial statements that comply with the requirements of different accounting regimes.

Where IFRS are being adopted, corporate bodies and accountants may experience the following:

- Companies will require a considerable input of accounting knowledge and experience to make the switch to IFRS.
- Considerable training will be required for accountants working within a company.
- Communications with other companies using IFRS will be improved.
- Business transactions should become easier.
- Auditing of multinational companies will be simpler.

One issue that is infrequently discussed is accounting education. Numerous studies have shown that, understandably, most accounting professors in the United States teach U.S. GAAP. Most of the textbooks, case studies, and other materials are based on U.S. GAAP. Although the requirements of IFRS are slowly appearing in some universities, any significant move to full adoption of international standards in the United States would require a huge change in U.S. accounting education.

Internationalization of accounting regulations has made progress, but the United States was not involved until 2002. A major study[19] was conducted for the Council of Institutional Investors in the United States. The Council opposed replacing U.S. accounting standards and standard setters with their international counterparts unless seven specific criteria were achieved.

The study explores evidence and views regarding each of the seven criteria. The criteria and the main conclusions are as follows:

**Criterion No. 1:** In the aggregate, information that results from application of IFRS is, at a minimum, of the same quality as the information resulting from U.S. accounting standards.

Findings. A majority of U.S. and European financial executives surveyed believe the quality of IFRS is high. Most also believe that the IASB and the U.S. FASB have made progress developing joint standards to address improvements needed prior to adoption of IFRS in all major capital markets.

**Criterion No. 2:** Application and enforcement of IFRS are at least as rigorous and consistent as U.S. accounting standards.

Findings. Research reveals a relationship between a country's institutional setting, including corporate governance and audit quality, and characteristics of a country's financial reporting.

**Criterion No. 3:** The IASB has sufficient resources including a secure and stable source of funding that is not dependent on voluntary contributions of those subject to the standards.

Findings. The IFRS Foundation, the parent entity of the IASB, is focused on moving as soon as possible to a funding source that relies on public sponsorship or other intermediated mechanisms. As of 2011, the United States is the only country where the IFRS

Foundation will seek direct corporate contributions. The IFRS Foundation's 2011 budget, released in April, projects a break-even year and indicates that direct contributions from U.S. companies (8 percent) and international accounting firms (26 percent) represent 34 percent of total projected revenues.

**Criterion No. 4:** The IASB has a full-time standard-setting Board and staff that are free of bias and possess the technical expertise necessary to fulfill their important roles.

Findings. Recent changes to the IASB's governing documents have elevated the importance of geographic representation as a criterion for serving on the Board (previously, technical expertise was the primary criterion). The changes also permit up to three part-time members of the Board.

**Criterion No. 5:** The IASB has demonstrated a clear recognition that investors are the key customers of audited financial reports and, therefore, the primary role of audited financial reports should be to satisfy in a timely manner investors' information needs. This includes having significant, prominent, and adequately balanced representation from qualified investors on the standard setter's staff, standard-setting Board, and oversight Board and outside monitoring or advisory groups.

Findings. The IFRS Foundation and the IASB have taken several steps to increase their focus on investors. Those steps include changes to the IASB's governing documents to designate investors as a major target audience, increasing investor representation in the standard-setting process, and enhancing investor outreach. Notwithstanding the progress that has been made to increase investor representation in the standard-setting process, only 5 of the present 20 seats on the IFRS Foundation, 8 of 47 seats on the IFRS Advisory Council (IFRS Council), and 3 of the 15 seats on the IASB are held by individuals from the investor community.

**Criterion No. 6:** The [IASB] has a thorough public due process that includes solicitation of investor input on proposals and careful consideration of investor views before issuing proposals or final standards.

Findings. Evidence is mixed about whether recent amendments to the IASB's governing documents are sufficient to improve due process. Nevertheless, in 2007, an independent think tank recognized the

IASB as possessing the best developed external stakeholder engagement capabilities among 30 of the world's most powerful global organizations.

**Criterion No. 7:** The IASB has a structure and process that adequately protect the standard setter's technical decisions and judgments (including the timing of the implementation of standards) from being overridden by government officials or bodies.

Findings. All organizations involved in standard setting face ongoing questions regarding their authority and responsibility. The IASB is no exception. To date, its technical decisions and judgments have been subject to significant pressures from governmental officials and bodies, particularly those representing the EU.

This is a thorough analysis of the situation but it must be remembered that the seven criteria were established by the Council of Institutional Investors in the United States. Other groups in other countries may have different criteria that they would wish to be satisfied.

## The U.S. Route to Convergence

The progress toward convergence from 2002 to 2014 was one of memorandums, road maps, objectives, and milestones. Despite all of these carefully worded documents, full convergence was not achieved and U.S. GAAP remains firmly in place, although definitely changed. The timeline of the progress that has taken place is summarized below.

### *2002—The Commencement of the Journey*

The Norwalk Agreement was signed.

### *2006—Issue of a Road map*

Both Boards affirmed their commitment toward making progress toward convergence. Instead of attempting to remove the differences in existing standards, they agreed that it would be more fruitful to develop new and high-quality standards. They also agreed to replace weaker standards with better ones and a number of objectives to be achieved by 2008 were agreed upon.

## *2007—Foreign Issuers Permitted to List Using IFRS*

In the light of the progress achieved by the Boards and other factors, the SEC adopted a final ruling in 2007.[20] This indicated the Commission's confidence that IFRS, as issued by the IASB, were robust enough to provide investors with reliable and relevant financial data. Some outsiders were quietly asking why U.S. companies could not use IFRS if they were acceptable from foreign issuers wishing to list on the NYSE.

## *2008—Issue of a Road map*

An update was issued to the 2006 document, which identified a series of priorities and milestones, emphasizing the goal of joint projects to produce common, principle-based standards. The 2008 IFRS road map indicated that adoption of IFRS in the United States would be conditional upon the achievement of progress toward these milestones:

- Improvements in accounting standards. The SEC was to continue to monitor the degree of progress made by the FASB and IASB regarding the development of accounting standards.
- Accountability and funding of the International Accounting Standards Committee Foundation (IASCF). The IASCF was required to show indications of securing stable funding that supported the independent functioning of the IASB.
- Improvement in the use of interactive data for IFRS reporting. The SEC mandated filings for public companies in the Extensible Business Reporting Language (XBRL) format. The mandate came into effect for the largest 500 U.S. companies for financial disclosures made after June 15, 2009.
- Education and training. The SEC was to consider the state of preparedness of U.S. issuers, auditors, and users, including the availability of IFRS education and training.

The 2008 Roadmap generally received applause. We reproduce below part of a synopsis from the influential Financial Reporting Policy

Committee of the Financial Accounting and Reporting Section of the American Accounting Association. The Committee stated:

> Based on a review of the literature, the AAA FRPC has concluded that a move to an international set of financial reporting standards is a desirable goal. We have also concluded that continued convergence of U.S. GAAP with IFRS by joint relations between the International Accounting Standards Board, hereafter IASB, and the Financial Accounting Standards Board, hereafter FASB, is preferable to near-term adoption of IFRS as a strategy for convergence. AAA FRC.[21]

### *2009—Pressure from Outside Bodies*

The financial crisis of 2007/2008 was largely blamed on the inadequacy of accounting regulations to determine the proper treatment of financial instruments. There were requests from many parties, including various government agencies, for the FASB and the IASB to speed up their progress. In response, the IASB and the FASB published a progress report describing an intensification of their work program, including the hosting of monthly joint Board meetings and to provide quarterly updates on their progress on convergence projects.

### *2010—Draft Strategic Plan Issued—Final Decision Set for 2011*

The SEC published its Draft Strategic Plan for fiscal years 2010 through 2015. The document includes drafts of the SEC's mission, vision, values, strategic goals, major initiatives, and performance metrics. In the plan, the SEC proposed an objective of promoting high-quality financial reporting worldwide through, among other things, support for a single set of high-quality global accounting standards and promotion of the ongoing convergence initiatives between the FASB and the IASB.[22]

The Plan also stated that the decision for incorporating IASs in the U.S. financial reporting system would be made in 2011. The document did not provide any details of potential transition dates or approaches, but the staff stated that 2015 or 2016 seemed reasonable based on comments received on the 2008 IFRS road map. The SEC also indicated that an early adoption was viable if it decided to make the use of IFRS mandatory.

### *2012—Joint Progress Report Issued*

The IASB and FASB published a joint progress document in which they described the progress made on an accounting standard for financial instruments. This included a joint expected loss impairment (provisioning) approach and a more converged approach to classification and measurement.

It was anticipated that the SEC would make a final decision on the time of full adoption of international accounting in 2012. It did not do so and the opinions of some other major players were that the IASB should cease its relationship with the United States and direct its attention to the rest of the world.

The Institute of Chartered Accountants in England and Wales responded to the failure of the SEC to decide on convergence and proposed that the convergence project should be ended formally, in months and not years. The argument was made that the IASB should concern itself with the 100-plus countries that had adopted international standards and assist those countries, such as China, which were making moves to convergence.[23]

The Chairman of the IASB, Hans Hoogervorst, is quoted as saying that "Five years ago, it (lack of U.S. adoption) might have led to a disintegration of the whole project. I am not worried about that now. But I am worried that the U.S. finds it so hard to make a decision and that it might lead to a growing divergence between IFRS and U.S. GAAP" (Perrin 2013).[24]

### *2013—Publishing of an Update*

The IASB and FASB published a high-level update on the status and timeline of the remaining convergence projects. The report includes an update on the impairment phase of the joint project on financial instruments.

## *2014—FASB Promotes Convergence*

The term international convergence of accounting standards may be interpreted in different ways. For some it might mean the discussion between two or more parties leading to complete agreement on one course of action.

The FASB argued in 2014 that the term refers to both the intended goal and the path by which to reach it and explains its strategy on its website:

- The FASB believes that, over time, the ultimate *goal* of convergence is the development of a unified set of high-quality IASs that companies worldwide would use for both domestic and cross-border financial reporting.
- Until that ultimate goal is achieved, the FASB is committed to working with other standard-setting bodies to develop accounting standards that are as converged as possible without forgoing the quality demanded by U.S. investors and other users of financial statements.
- From 2002 to 2013, the *path* toward convergence has been the collaborative efforts of the FASB and the IASB to both *improve* U.S. GAAP and IFRS *and eliminate or minimize the differences between them.*
- As the FASB and the IASB complete their work on the last of their joint standard-setting projects initially undertaken under the 2006 Memorandum of Understanding (MoU), the process will evolve to include cooperation and collaboration among a wider range of standard setters around the world.
- Moving forward, the FASB will continue to work on global accounting issues with the IASB through its membership in the Accounting Standards Advisory Forum, a newly established advisory body comprising 12 standard setters from across the globe.
- For issues of primary interest to stakeholders in U.S. capital markets, the FASB will set its own agenda. As the FASB initiates its own new projects based on feedback from its stakeholders, it will reach out to all who have an interest in improving financial reporting for companies and investors that participate in U.S. capital markets, including U.S. capital market stakeholders who live and work outside the United States.

Although the above statement emphasizes involvement in international matters, it is evident that there is no intention to converge fully the FASB and the IASB standards. It is also clear that there is no enthusiasm for the FASB withdrawing from its role as the sole standard setter in the United States. Such a stance is not surprising given the role and importance of the SEC and the different conceptual approaches to establishing accounting regulations.

There were criticisms within the United States of the FASB's continual pursuit of convergence. Miller and Bahnson[25] argued that the FASB should reform standards and practices in the United States, thus leading the world by example. They considered that the efforts to converge were a waste of resources and that it was impossible to develop high-quality standards in partnership with the IASB. Unfortunately, the definition of high quality has been elusive and, we would argue, is enmeshed with the principles- and rules-based approach to standard setting. We address these subjects in the next two sections of this chapter.

## High-Quality Standards

It is not surprising that members of all interested parties would claim to support high-quality standards. Unfortunately, nobody has been able to define what is meant by the term, although some have explained the characteristics of such standards.

In 1997, the then Chair of the SEC claimed that standards must result in comparability and transparency, and provide for full disclosure. Investors must be able to meaningfully analyze performance across time periods and among companies. Of course, one main aim of IASs is to ensure comparability of companies' financial results at the international level.

The SEC[26] echoes the words of many others when it states that high-quality accounting standards consist of a comprehensive set of neutral principles that require consistent, comparable, relevant, and reliable information. It believes that the information should be useful for investors, lenders, creditors, and others who make capital allocation decisions.

The IASB shares the same sentiments as the others. With so much agreement on the need for high-quality standards it is confusing that convergence did not take place years ago. One reason may be that the phrases used are descriptive and also avoid the tougher issues.

For example, high-quality standards should have relevance and reliability. It can sometimes be difficult to combine these two characteristics. Let us assume that I bought a house for $250,000 some years ago and I am now seeking a bank loan. I tell the manager that my house has a current market value of $350,000. Does the manager take the reliable value of $250,000 or the value relevant to his decision, which may not be reliable? Mostly, in preparing financial statements, accountants use the reliable or historic values. We discussed this in Chapter 1.

Given the difficulties in defining high-quality standards, there are several questions that need to be addressed:

1. What are high-quality standards? The present description of characteristics such as relevance and reliability does not help.
2. What is the purpose of high-quality accounting standards? The answer must be high-quality financial statements. This, however, requires not only good standards but a process of interpretation, monitoring, and enforcement to ensure companies comply.
3. How do we measure high quality?

Some of these questions have been answered by a research study, Barth,[27] that compared characteristics of accounting amounts for firms that apply IASs to a matched sample of firms that do not. Measures of accounting quality used earnings management, timely loss recognition, and value relevance metrics.

The results showed that firms applying international standards use less earnings management, more timely loss recognition, and more value relevance of accounting amounts than do those applying domestic GAAP. The conclusion from the study suggests that improvement in accounting quality is associated with applying IAS.

Of course, one study does not provide complete answers. But it does emphasize that the pursuit of high-quality standards requires some measures by which we can assess them. It must also be accepted that standards are not only driven by technical accounting considerations but other powerful influences.

In 2017, the Chair of the SEC (White 2017)[28] stressed the need for high-quality standards that are globally accepted. U.S. investors make investment decisions in foreign companies that are using international standards. U.S. companies make acquisitions, enter into joint ventures, and enter into transactions with foreign companies that use international standards. Although the convergence project had come to an end, the SEC should continue its collaboration with the IASB. Unfortunately, it does not seem that the two Boards have a shared definition of "high quality" and we discuss the cause of this divide in the next section.

## Principles Based versus Rules Based

If international accounting is to be achieved, there must be agreement on the assumptions and concepts that are to serve as the basis for setting standards. Unfortunately, the IASB has a very different starting position on the subject compared to that of the United States. The IASB uses a principles-based approach to standard setting; the United States uses a rules-based approach.

The difference between a principles-based approach and a rules-based approach is that the former applies detailed requirements to ensure that financial statements are not misleading. With the principles-based approach, the burden is placed on the preparers and auditors of the financial statements to use their professional judgment and experience to ensure that the financial statements are not misleading and comply with the conceptual regulations in the standards.

The rules-based approach holds that by following the rules strictly when preparing financial statements, such statements will give faithful representation. The main characteristic of a rules-based approach is that the regulations set out specific criteria, *bright line* thresholds, examples, scope restrictions, exceptions, subsequent precedents, and implementation guidance (Nelson 2003).[29]

In Chapter 4, we discuss accounting for leasing. At this stage we summarize below the main requirements of the U.S. standards and the international accounting guidance on determining what constitutes a lease. Both standards concentrate on what is a capital (finance) lease and this must be shown on the balance sheet.

The original U.S. standard (SFAS 13) defines a capital lease as one under which any one of the following four conditions is met:

1. The present value at the beginning of the lease term of the payments, not representing executory costs, paid by the lessor equals or exceeds 90 percent of the fair value of the leased asset;
2. The lease transfers ownership of the asset to the lessee by the end of the lease term;
3. The lease contains a bargain purchase price;
4. The lease is equal to 75 percent or more of the estimated economic life of the leased asset.

It does not require much ingenuity by directors and accountants to draw up a contract where the percentages fall on the most advantageous side for the company and the information it wishes to disclose.

The former international standard, Accounting for Leases (IAS 17), states that the classification of a lease depends on the *substance* of the transaction, rather than the *form.* The standard describes situations that would normally lead a lease to be classified as a financing (capital) lease, and these include the following:

- The lease transfers ownership of the asset to the lessee by the end of the lease term;
- The lessee has the option to purchase the asset at a price that is expected to be sufficiently lower than the fair value at the date the option becomes exercisable that, at the inception of the lease, it is reasonably certain that the option will be exercised;
- The lease term is for the major part of the economic life of the asset, even if the title is not transferred;
- At the inception of the lease, the present value of the minimum lease payments amounts to at least substantially all of the fair value of the leased asset; and
- The leased assets are of a specialized nature such that only the lessee can use them without major modifications being made.

The above examples demonstrate the rules-based approach with its specific, quantitative guidelines, and the principles-based approach with its descriptive guidance. One might conclude that more stringent rules would ensure that companies would properly define a lease as a capital lease rather than an operating lease, which does not have to appear on the balance sheet. This does not, however, always occur. Research[30] has shown that firms that follow U.S. GAAP and use a lease standard that contains bright line rules are more likely to classify leases as operating than firms that utilize IFRS and adhere to a principles-based standard.

The problem with adhering strictly to specified rules is that it excludes professional judgment. This can result in decisions that are consistent with the rules but inconsistent with the principle of providing the most useful financial information to users. If the rules are very specific, such as in the U.S. regulations on leasing, companies may be able to arrange their activities so that they comply and fall within the rules, but the financial statements still remain misleading. This action may be outside legal criticism, but may stretch the limits of what is permissible under the law, and may not be ethically or morally acceptable—or even contribute to good accounting.

Conversely, it can be argued that the principles-based approach gives too much scope to preparers and auditors, which creates opportunities for creative accounting. Without clear guidance on how to account for a transaction, several methods may be considered acceptable. Those different methods can lead to different answers, which is not in the best interests of the users of financial statements.

Additionally, if there are no clear rules, individual companies may choose different accounting treatments for the same transaction and the characteristic of comparability will be lost. It is difficult to compare the financial results of companies if they use different methods to account for transactions and events. A main argument in favor of international accounting is that it permits the comparability of financial statements from multiple jurisdictions.

The principles approach of the IASB may have been influenced by the long-held tenet in the United Kingdom that financial statements should give a true and fair view. The concept of a true and fair view first appeared in the United Kingdom in the Joint Stock Companies

Registration and Regulation Act of 1844[31] and over the years, there has been debate over its meaning.

In 2005, the Financial Reporting Council[32] in the United Kingdom confirmed that, following the adoption of IAS 1 and *fair presentation* in the EU, the concept of *true and fair view* remained a cornerstone of financial reporting and auditing in the United Kingdom.

In 2012, this position has been reconfirmed by the Financial Reporting Council[33] and the consequences of its application explained:

> Para 18—The requirement to give a true and fair view may in special circumstances require a departure from accounting standards. However, because accounting standards are formulated with the objective of ensuring that the information resulting from their application faithfully represents the underlying commercial activity, the FRC envisages that only in exceptional circumstances will departure from the requirements of an accounting standard be necessary in order for financial statements to give a true and fair view.
>
> Para 19—If in extremely rare circumstances compliance with the requirements of an accounting standard is inconsistent with the requirement to give a true and fair view, the requirements of the accounting standard should be departed from to the extent necessary to give a true and fair view.

Although IAS 1 used the term financial presentation, the ability to override the requirements of accounting standards was maintained, although some argued that its interpretation was very different from true and fair. Evans (2003)[34] critically examined the evidence and concluded that the override in IAS 1 should be viewed in its narrowest possible interpretation, and not as an independent and all-pervasive fundamental concept.

Subsequent articles have pursued this debate and widened it to philosophical discussions.[35] Unfortunately, whatever the approach the debate has not achieved a conclusive answer.

Given the above background, it is not surprising that the debate on the principles-based versus rules-based approach is so heated, and one can appreciate the problems that some countries confront in adopting IASs completely. The United States has a very strong rules-based approach.

It is almost impossible to envisage that approach being overturned. It is also unlikely that the FASB will depart from its position. It is therefore extremely difficult to envisage the FASB and the IASB reaching a stage where the differences between those two approaches are no longer considered important.

## Conclusion

The issues in continuing with national accounting regulations in a world where business activities are becoming increasingly international in nature had become apparent toward the second half of the 20th century. The solution appeared to be IASs where the emphasis would be on high quality and the objective would be the comparability of financial statements, no matter the country in which the company operated.

Unfortunately, although the barriers toward countries adopting international standards have been identified, the success in removing these barriers has been difficult to attain. The IASC had achieved some success in harmonizing accounting practices, and since 2001, the IASB can claim to have significantly advanced the cause of internationalization. However, the United States has not adopted IASs.

There has been considerable joint effort by the FASB and the IASB to achieve converged standards. Starting with the Norwalk Agreement in 2002, the parties have expended considerable resources in attempting to agree to the regulations. There have been several successes which have led to improvements in accounting regulations internationally. However, it would seem that the hurdles have been too great and the involvement of the United States declined from 2012 until there was complete withdrawal in 2014.

In this chapter we have linked two issues that have prevented full convergence: high-quality standards and the rules-based approach versus the principles-based approach to establishing accounting regulations. Although there is complete agreement that the search is for high quality, what is meant by this term remains elusive. It appears, however, that the FASB would appear to favor a standard that has a strong rules-based foundation, whereas the IASB is more inclined to set out the underlying principles. There is no apparent easy way to bridge this gap so full convergence will not be achieved.

It is unthinkable that the United States will turn its back completely on international standards, but the road that it has chosen is one of partial convergence. The stance that the FASB is taking is clearly stated on its website:

> The FASB believes that pursuing convergence—making global accounting standards as similar as possible—is fully consistent with that mission. Investors, companies, auditors, and other participants in the U.S. financial reporting system should benefit from the increased comparability that would result from internationally converged accounting standards. More comparable standards would reduce costs to both users and preparers of financial statements and make worldwide capital markets more efficient (FASB).[36]

This is sound support for continuing a dialogue and, despite the events in 2012, it appears as if the United States intends to continue its international involvement. It is impossible to predict whether full convergence will be achieved. Our opinion is that the combined work to produce high-quality standards will continue, but where agreement on particular issues cannot be agreed, the two Boards will make their own decisions. The result will be that U.S. GAAP is *similar* to international standards but will have altered the original requirements. However, it will remain as U.S. GAAP controlled by the SEC and the FASB, and will *not* be fully compatible with international standards as issued by the IASB.

# CHAPTER 4
# Standards of Dissent

## About This Chapter

Accounting regulations are not static. Although the FASB and the IASB issue standards, they are subject to subsequent amendments irrespective of the progress of the convergence project. Accounting standard setters are continuously monitoring company practices and issue revised or new standards where there are perceived deficiencies.

Sometimes there are new business practices to be regulated, or political and legal decisions made at the national level that require a new standard or amendments to an existing one. Not surprisingly, the process of convergence becomes entangled with these political and legal influences.

We make no judgments as to whether the convergence efforts successfully resolve these issues. As we stated above, standards change for various reasons and some of these may be country specific. What we illustrate in this chapter is the complexity of attempting to achieve convergence.

In addition to converging the requirements of a standard, there is also the application of that standard to be considered. The question arises as to whether the financial statements capture the full intention of the standard. Auditors in the EU have to ensure that financial statements comply with their understanding of the requirements of International Financial Reporting Standards (IFRS). In the United States auditors have to ensure that the financial statements comply with the regulations in that country as converged with IFRSs. As discussed in the previous chapter, there are questions on the completeness of convergence. It is possible that the EU and U.S. auditors, through their years of training and experience, have differing interpretations of the requirements. This chapter demonstrates that the complexity of the regulations may lead to differing interpretations.

In this chapter we look at some major issues that have confronted the standard setters in their search for convergence. The examples involve politics, business practices, and technical accounting considerations. In our discussions we concentrate on explaining the issues that confronted the standard setters, rather than a detailed analysis of the accounting requirements. The issues we discuss are:

- Revenue recognition
- Inventory valuation
- Stock-based payments
- Leasing
- Intangible assets
- Financial instruments

With each of these standards, we provide a brief history of the international standard to set the scene for the discussion on its requirements.

## Legislation, Politics, and Convergence

Financial accounting is regulated not only by accounting standards, but also by other legislation that applies to companies and therefore impacts on the financial information they publicly disclose. Each country has its own government structure that regulates the operation of its organizations. In the United Kingdom the Financial Reporting Council (FRC) has the authority to determine the information, both financial and nonfinancial, that companies should disclose and this includes compliance with international accounting standards. The FRC is also responsible for ensuring that the Companies Act 2006, a significant and substantial document, is adhered to by all companies registered in the United Kingdom.

A significant piece of legislation passed in the United States was the Sarbanes–Oxley (SOX) Act of 2002. This was a regulatory response to the large financial frauds and accounting irregularities that had occurred in companies such as Enron, WorldCom, and Tyco.

The SOX Act generally applies to U.S. and non-U.S. public companies. The requirements of the Act that are particularly relevant to this book are as follows:

- The chief executive officer (CEO) and chief financial officer (CFO) are responsible for signing off their company's financial statements and indicating that the financial statements do not omit material information.
- The CEO and CFO must indicate that they are responsible for the company's system of internal controls over financial reporting.
- The Public Accounting Oversight Board was established to oversee the audit of public companies.
- Listed companies must have a majority of independent directors and there must be regular meetings scheduled with managers of the company.

The SOX Act is possibly the most substantial legislation passed in the United States addressing financial accounting and reporting, and corporate governance for many decades. There have been criticisms that it places too large a burden on companies but, given the extent of the corporate misbehaviors that were taking place in the early 2000s, the government was compelled to take action.

Attempting to converge U.S. GAAP and IFRS, therefore, is not only about technical accounting. Indeed, it is sometimes less about technicalities and more about politics. Although the Securities and Exchange Commission (SEC) may be extremely powerful, it is still exposed to lobbying, arguments, persuasions, and criticisms. As the direct standard setter, the FASB has the same pressures, plus it is also answerable to the SEC.

The IASB, in some ways, is in an even more difficult position than the FASB as it is unable to enforce its standards. They must rely on the assumption that the countries adopting international accounting standards are in agreement with the regulations and will be diligent in ensuing that companies comply with the standards. There have been extensive discussions and debates over the issues surrounding enforcement and adoption of standards, but this is not the responsibility of the IASB. The IASB does, however, have an advantage over the FASB as it does not have a legal obligation to issue standards on any particular area of accounting.

Although technical accounting issues need to be addressed, both the FASB and the IASB must be receptive to the opinions of their constituents while trying to achieve convergence. Possibly, the best example of the two Boards working together was the joint revenue project. But even with this apparent success it has been argued that "History has shown from previous convergence efforts that even when the standards are identical, practice in the United States can differ from practice under IFRSs" (Holzmann and Hunter 2015, 105[1]).

It would also be fair to say that for the most part, standards do not lead to new business developments, but follow them. The FASB and the IASB attempt to identify developments at their early stages and introduce standards to regulate them. That they are not always successful in fully converging their efforts is illustrated in the following examples discussed in this chapter.

## Revenue Recognition

### *History of Standard*

| | |
|---|---|
| January 1, 1984 | IAS 18 Revenue recognition come into effect |
| December 1993 | Revisions |
| December 1998 | Amended |
| April 2007 | Amended |
| January 1, 2018 | Superseded by IFRS 15 Revenue from Contracts with Customers |

To calculate the profit or loss of a company for a financial period, we need to know the revenue from the transactions that were carried out by an organization in that period—that is, the sale of goods or services. This calculation can be far more difficult than individuals may realize. There are several factors that have an impact on the calculation of revenue and its effect on the income statement, which shows the profit or loss.

First, financial statements (apart from the cash flow statement) must be prepared on the accruals basis. This means that transactions and other events are recognized as they occur and not when cash or other equivalents, such as checks, are actually given or received. In other words, transactions are recorded when they are entered into, not at the time of the cash inflow or outflow. This rule applies in both accounting for revenue and the expenses generated in achieving it. The following straightforward example demonstrates the issues that can arise:

### *Example of Revenue Recognition*

On March 1, an auto dealer buys a preowned Jaguar car for $30,000. He pays for the Jaguar immediately and fully in cash. The dealer subsequently discovers that the car, once some work has been done on it, can be considered a collector's item. The work is completed by an associate for $10,000, which the dealer has to pay by the end of April. The dealer sells the car by the end of March for $60,000. The buyer pays a deposit of $15,000 by check and promises to pay the remaining balance in June.

Looking at the month of March, when applying the accruals basis of accounting, profit is calculated as follows:

| | $ | $ |
|---|---|---|
| Revenue | | 60,000 |
| Cost of car | 30,000 | |
| Repair work | 10,000 | 40,000 |
| Profit | | 20,000 |

There may be a major problem for the dealer as he has paid $30,000 for the car, but has only received $15,000 toward the sale. There is a cash deficit. There are also some uncertainties with the profit. Suppose the associate who did the repairs also worked on some other of the auto dealer's vehicles at the same time, and these repairs were all included in the total bill for $10,000. How much of the $10,000 relates to the Jaguar?

Suppose that the buyer finds a problem with the car—will the dealer be expected to correct it free of charge? If the dealer goes out of business and disappears, how do we record the $10,000 of expenses? If the check for $15,000 is dishonored, how do we account for it and how does that impact on the total revenue?

The scenario above is a very simple example; in many businesses, transactions are far more complex:

- Customers may purchase several items over a period of time, but wish to pay for everything at one date, or in a series of installments.
- Costs can be incurred before the sale takes place, during the transaction, and sometime after. Payment can be immediate, delayed, or never made.
- Customers may require credit.
- The supplier may offer interest-free credit, but how does this affect the revenue and costs?
- The sale may cover two or more financial periods.
- If a service is offered, such as a maintenance contract, it could be for several years, although the customer pays the full amount in the first year. How is the payment recorded?

Both U.S. GAAP and IFRS had regulations on revenue recognition that were sometimes difficult to apply. There were also considerable differences between their respective approaches. In addition to the two approaches being different, it was acknowledged that with existing regulations there were opportunities for unscrupulous companies to massage their revenues. The companies could either accelerate the revenue into an earlier financial period or delay it into a later one.

Understandably, the topic of revenue recognition was an important regulation to address by the FASB and the IASB. It was an issue that required attention and appeared to offer an opportunity to develop a common standard for U.S. GAAP and IFRS that would:

1. Remove inconsistencies and weaknesses in existing revenue requirements.
2. Provide a more robust framework for addressing revenue issues.
3. Improve comparability of revenue recognition practices across entities, industries, jurisdictions, and capital markets.
4. Provide more useful information to users of financial statements through improved disclosure requirements.
5. Simplify the preparation of financial statements by reducing the number of requirements to which an entity must refer.

The attempts to converge standards took many years. Finally, in 2014 the FASB and IASB each separately issued their final standards on revenue from contracts with customers. The standards were issued as ASU 2014-09 (codified in ASC 606) by the FASB and as IFRS 15, *Revenue From Contracts With Customers*, by the IASB. Both the FASB and the IASB requirements are effective in 2018.

IFRS 15 uses a five-step model and, in general, these are consistent and straightforward regardless of industry. The U.S. regulations identify whether a sale is realized or realizable and then whether it has been earned. The requirements depart from the international standard as there is a list of rules specific to the industry in which the business operates.

The research and comments on the impact of the new U.S. standard suggest that its effect will not be substantial and may be limited to certain industries. A survey of over 700 executives conducted in 2016 by PwC and Financial Executives Research Foundation (FERF)[2] found that 64 percent of respondents did not expect the standard to have a material impact on the income statement and balance sheet, 20 percent were unsure, and 16 percent did expect a material impact. The argument has been made by Rutledge, Karim and Kim[3] that the major impact will be on income tax expenses and deferred taxes.

Although there has been substantial convergence with revenue recognition, there remain some differences in the regulations. These may not appear major when comparing the wording of the two standards but could be significant when interpreted and applied to actual transactions.

One issue is the different definitions used in the two standards to define the word probable. The FASB definition is that "future event or events are likely to occur". IAS 37 is the international standard defining probable and it considers that the term means that "the event is more likely than not to occur, i.e. the probability that the event will occur is greater that the probability that it will not."

These are small linguistic differences but one study[4] using students for the experiment gave them either FASB or IFRS definition of "probable" and asked them to evaluate five revenue recognition scenarios. Their findings showed that the differences in the definitions did not lead to differences in application of the requirements of the standards. Although this allays some concerns, it is difficult to predict whether opinions in the lecture theater are transferable to the business arena.

Understandably, the main preoccupation in the U.S. literature is concerned with the changes in the new U.S. standard compared to the old standards. It has been suggested that the new U.S. revenue recognition standard may decrease earnings quality because there is more scope for management judgment. If this is the case, there may be more differences in the application of the "converged" standards than were anticipated.

## Inventory Valuation

### *History of Standard*

| | |
|---|---|
| October 1975 | IAS 2 Inventories issued |
| December 1993 | IAS 9 issued |
| December 18, 2003 | IAS 2 issued |
| January 1, 2005 | IAS 2 Revised comes into effect |

Closing inventory valuation is an extremely important subject as it is a key item in the calculation of profit and it informs the reader of the financial statement of the value of inventory at the company's fiscal year-end. Inventory includes all of the costs incurred in purchasing merchandise and preparing it for sale. This includes raw materials, direct labor, and manufacturing overhead. Inventory values at the year-end can be substantial; we will demonstrate this fact through the example of General Electric (GE).

| December 31 (in millions, U.S. $) | 2016 | 2015 |
|---|---|---|
| Raw materials and work in progress | 12,636 | 13,415 |
| Finished goods | 8,798 | 8,265 |
| Unbilled shipments | 536 | 628 |
| | 21,971 | 22,308 |
| Less revaluations to last-in, first-out | 383 | 207 |
| Total inventories | 22,354 | 22,515 |

*Source:* GE Annual Report 2016, 156.

The cost for a significant portion of GE's U.S. inventories is determined on a last-in, first-out (LIFO) basis: a method allowed in the United States but not under the international accounting standard. The cost of other GE inventories is determined on a first-in, first-out (FIFO) basis, which is a U.S. and international permitted method.

Given the substantial dollar amounts, it is essential that we understand the impact of a change in valuation methods. A very simple example will demonstrate the calculation of gross profit and the critical importance of inventory valuation.

**Example**

A merchandising company imports shoes at a cost of U.S. $10 each and sells them at U.S. $20 each. In January 2017, the number of shoes it purchased and sold is:

| | | |
|---|---|---|
| Number imported: 100 | | |
| Number sold: 90 | | |
| Calculation of gross profit for January | $ | $ |
| Revenue (90 @ $20) | | 1,800 |
| *Cost of goods sold* | | |
| Purchases (100 @ $10) | 1,000 | |
| Deduct closing inventory (10 @ $10) | 100 | 900 |
| Gross profit | | 900 |

With this simple model, it is easy to calculate that a gross profit of U.S. $10 is made on each sneaker. If the company sells 90 of its products, the gross profit must be U.S. $900. The critical factor is the inventory or stock taking, which is conducted at the end of January. It is imperative to ensure that the closing inventory of 10 shoes is physically being held by the company. If the actual count of inventory is less than 10, this variance is an indication of an error, whether due to misappropriation of assets or disposals due to damage. If this is the case, then the closing inventory will be lower and the gross profit will therefore also be lower.

Having confirmed that 10 shoes are indeed in closing inventory, the next question is how they are to be valued. In the above example, valuation would be at the cost of U.S. $10. Problems will arise if the cost of shoes increases. Let us assume that the information for February is the same as that for January, except that the supplier has increased the cost of the shoes to U.S. $15.

The question is how do we value the closing inventory of 20 shoes? There are several ways to do so, but the dispute occurs between two main options.

1. We can assume that we sold the last shoes that came in February first. Therefore, of the 100 shoes that came in February, we have 10 remaining at U.S. $15 and we still have the 10 from January at a cost of U.S. $10—total U.S. $250. This is known as the LIFO method.
2. We can assume that in February, we first sold the 10 remaining shoes that had cost U.S. $10 each. The 20 shoes remaining therefore were all purchased in February at U.S. $15—total U.S. $300. This is known as the FIFO method.

The method that is chosen has a significant impact on gross profit. Table 4.1 shows the results for February using both methods.

Under the LIFO method, the value of the closing inventory is lower and therefore the accounting calculation of the costs of goods sold is higher than that of the FIFO method. As the profit is lower, the company will pay less income tax. The difference between the cost of an inventory calculated under the FIFO and LIFO methods is called the LIFO reserve. This reserve is essentially the amount by which an entity's taxable income has been deferred by using the LIFO method. Of course, this is only true when the costs of purchases are increasing. If the purchase price declines the opposite results would occur.

***Table 4.1 LIFO and FIFO comparison***

| | LIFO | | FIFO | |
|---|---|---|---|---|
| Revenue | | 1,800 | | 1,800 |
| Opening inventory | 100 | | 100 | |
| Purchases | 1,500 | | 1,500 | |
| | 1,600 | | 1,600 | |
| **Less** closing inventory | 250 | 1,350 | 300 | 1,300 |
| Gross profit | | 450 | | 500 |

FIFO, first-in, first-out; LIFO, last-in, first-out.

For some companies, the different use of the inventory valuation method has little impact. There are also examples where separate parts of the business use alternative methods, such as the case with Walmart.

## Inventories

We value inventories at the lower of cost or market as determined primarily by the retail method of accounting, using the last-in, first-out ("LIFO") method for substantially all of the Walmart U.S. segment's inventories. The inventory at the Walmart International segment is valued primarily by the retail inventory method of accounting, using the first-in, first-out ("FIFO") method. The retail method of accounting results in inventory being valued at the lower of cost or market since permanent markdowns are immediately recorded as a reduction of the retail value of inventory. The inventory at the Sam's Club segment is valued using the LIFO method.
*Source:* Walmart Annual Report 2017, 33.

Not only does Walmart use both LIFO and FIFO, the weighted-average method is also used as it is permitted under both U.S. regulations and international standards. Walmart applies the retail inventory method of accounting, which is allowed in the United States and is in accordance with international standards.

Accounting for inventory in high-volume retail operations raises problems. It is difficult to determine the cost of each sale. The retail method, which is widely used, compiles the inventories at retail prices. In most retail entities, an observable pattern between cost and price exists. Retail prices can therefore be converted to cost through use of a formula.

The sales for the period are deducted from the retail value of the goods available for sale, to produce an estimated inventory at retail value. The ratio of cost to retail for all goods passing through a department or firm is then determined by dividing the total goods available for sale at cost by the total goods available at retail. The inventory valued at retail is converted to ending inventory at cost by applying the cost-to-retail ratio.

In the United States, the LIFO method has been an acceptable, popular accounting method since its inception in 1939 and is permitted for tax purposes. It is claimed that Congress believed that companies would not adopt it because it lowered profits, but the added effect of lowering taxes was too great an attraction for many companies.[5]

The tax advantages associated with LIFO have been documented by tax laws, research, literature, and Congress. The advantage is substantial in some industries and has led to the criticism of LIFO resulting in an unfair tax loophole for a few beneficial industries.[6]

Criticisms of LIFO have gathered strength and as part of the convergence project, it seemed that LIFO would be abolished so as to fall in line with the IFRS that prohibits LIFO as an acceptable method. The Obama administration proposed in its 2010 budget to repeal LIFO in the future, but there were signs that such a move would meet considerable opposition.[7]

Although there is resistance to the repeal of LIFO, there is evidence that some companies are voluntarily abandoning this method of valuing inventories. The number of public companies reporting LIFO reserves exceeded 1,000 from the late 1970s to the late 1980s. The tax advantage of LIFO is dependent on the presence of inflation, and the number of U.S. companies reporting a LIFO reserve decreased over the 5 years 2004–2008 as shown in Table 4.2.[8]

LIFO has been a method of valuing in the United States for nearly 100 years. The decision by the IASB to ban LIFO contributed to the calls within the United States to ban it. A recent article[9] found that organizations in the oil and manufacturing industries have significant LIFO reserves whereas organizations in high-tech and health industries were less likely to adopt LIFO.

***Table 4.2 Number of companies reporting LIFO reserves, 2004 to 2008***

| | 2004 | 2005 | 2006 | 2007 | 2008 |
|---|---|---|---|---|---|
| Companies with inventory balances at the year-end | 5,673 | 5,489 | 5,301 | 5,072 | 4,783 |
| Companies with inventory balances and LIFO reserves at year-end | 449 | 420 | 401 | 369 | 339 |
| Percent of companies with inventory balance and LIFO reserve at year-end | 7.91 | 7.65 | 7.56 | 7.28 | 7.09 |

## Stock-Based Payments (Share-Based in the International Standard)

### *History of Standard*

| | |
|---|---|
| January 1, 2005 | IFRS 2 Share-based payments effective |
| January 1, 2009 | Amendments |
| July 1, 2009 | Amendments |
| January 1, 2010 | Amendments |
| July 1, 2014 | Amendments |
| January 1, 2018 | Amendments |

The concept of share-based payments in IFRS 2 encompasses the issuance of shares, or rights to shares, in return for services and goods. This term covers several different types of transactions, but we will restrict our discussions to schemes that are designed for the benefit of employees, particularly directors (share options).

The price the company sets on the share (called the *grant* or *strike price*) is usually the market price of the share at the time the employee is given the options. Since those options cannot be exercised for some time, the hope of the lucky recipient is that the price of the shares will go up, so that selling them later at a higher market price will yield a profit. Definitions of some of the terms we use will be helpful.

### *Definitions*

*Stock options (UK "Share options"):* A benefit, given or sold by one party to another (in this case the employee), which gives the recipient the right, but not the obligation, to buy (call) or sell (put) a stock at an agreed-upon price within a certain period or on a specific date.

*Strike price*: The price at which the holder of a stock option may purchase the stock.

*Vesting*: When employees are given stock options, they usually do not gain control over the stock or options for a period of time. This period is known as the vesting period and is usually 3 to 5 years.

During the vesting period, the employee cannot sell or transfer the stock or options.

*Stock option expensing*: The method of accounting for the value of stock options on the income statement.

*Expiration date*: The date by which you must exercise your options.

*At the money stock options*: The stock option's strike price is *identical* to the prevailing market price.

*In the money stock options*: The stock option's grant or strike price is *lower* than the prevailing market price.

An example of a stock option is as follows: The recipient receives options on 1,000 shares of company stock. The vesting period is spread over 5 years, with one-fifth of the stock vested each year. The recipient can buy 200 shares each year at the strike price, and if so wishes can sell the shares at the current market price.

There is considerable, and often heated, debate as to whether stock options should be permitted. There are those who argue that the issuance of options aligns executives' interests with those of the company, increasing motivation and improving corporate performance. Others claim that it is merely a method of secretly siphoning off money to directors who are already handsomely rewarded.

### The Debates

One important aspect of the U.S. debate is stock optioning expensing—in other words, how companies should account for the options. In 1972, a new revision in U.S. GAAP meant that companies did not have to report executive incomes as an expense to their shareholders if the income resulted from an issuance of the money stock options. The result was that organizations reported higher profits and directors benefited without the full knowledge of shareholders.

There was an increasing growth in the use of stock options by companies and research indicated that in 2002, profit at technology firms in the S&P 500 would drop by 70 percent if they expensed options on the income statement. In utility organizations, the drop would only be

2 percent.[10] The pressure was on for stock options to be expensed, but there were political hurdles preventing this regulation.

It was not until March 31, 2004, that the FASB issued its long-awaited Exposure Draft, *Share-Based Payments.* Congress became involved with the draft and a bill was put before Congress in 2004 to limit stock option expense reported in the statements to the top five officers.[11]

Subsequent research[12] of the events in 2004 found that employee stock option expense under the bill before Congress would only be approximately 2 percent of what it would be under the FASB's preferred method. The research also reports that political connections and business interests were influencing the debate in Congress.

In December 2004, the FASB published FASB Statement 123 (Revised 2004): *Share-Based Payment.* This required that the compensation cost relating to share-based payment transactions be recognized in financial statements. It took the Board 2 years to develop a revised standard that provided investors and other users of financial information with more complete and neutral financial information (FASB 2004).[13] While Statement 123(R) is largely consistent with IFRS 2, some differences remain, as described in a Q&A document that FASB issued along with the new Statement.

IFRS 2 was originally issued by the IASB in February 2004 and first applied to annual periods beginning on or after January 1, 2005. The standard requires an entity to recognize share-based payment transactions (such as granted shares, share options, or share appreciation rights) in its financial statements, including transactions with employees or other parties that are to be settled in cash, other assets, or equity instruments of the entity. Specific requirements are included for equity-settled and cash-settled share-based payment transactions, as well as those transactions where the entity or supplier has a choice of cash or equity instruments.

The key provision of U.S. and international regulations is for public entities to recognize the fair value of the compensation cost for vested employees over their service period.

Critics could claim that the two Boards were unable to reach full convergence on this topic. However, given the many problems faced by the FASB, the reasonable response is that these accounting transactions were poorly regulated and a substantial degree of convergence has been achieved. Both U.S. GAAP and IFRS have issued standards over stock-based compensation.

The discussion above has been about accounting for stock options, from a technical accounting and convergence viewpoint. It is illuminating to look at business practices where the accounting regulations are not sufficiently clear. Stock options are a good example of a case where questionable (or even fraudulent) activities may be conducted by directors of a company.

With regard to stock options, two courses of action were taken that were of benefit to the directors receiving stock options. One of these was backdating, where option granting dates were retrospectively set to precede a rally in the underlying shares, locking in risk-free profits for recipients. The second is referred to as spring-loading, where grant dates are scheduled for just before a positive announcement or just after a negative one, anticipating a stock price rally and, therefore, resulting in higher profits for recipients.

The two practices above are not illegal, but must be properly disclosed in regulatory filings, taxed and reported on the accounting ledger. There is also a measure of control under the Sarbanes–Oxley Act that reduced the time that companies are required to report their options grants to the SEC from 30 days to 2 business days.

It is always difficult to state the extent of questionable behavior. One study by Persons[14] took a sample of 111 fraudulent companies and 111 matched nonfraudulent companies. The results indicated a significantly positive association between director stock-option compensation and the likelihood of fraud. On the other hand, there is no association between the fraud likelihood and independent directors' cash compensation and stock ownership.

The academic study conducted above does not reveal the financial impact of these questionable activities. In June 2007, in a report Swanton[15] examining the involvement of general counsels (GC) stated that the SEC:

- Brought civil fraud charges against Nancy Heinen, former GC of Apple, for her involvement in backdating stock options.
- Filed a civil complaint against former Amkor Technology GC Kevin Heron for alleged insider trading. A federal grand jury

previously indicted Heron on four counts of securities fraud for the same activities. Heron allegedly netted U.S. $290,000 from the illegal trades.

- D Marvell Technology Group announced the termination of Matthew Gloss, GC of its U.S. operating subsidiary.
- The company did not say why Gloss was terminated, but did say that it would take a U.S. $350,000 charge related to stock options backdating.
- D Amtel Corp. released the results of an internal investigation that found former GC Mike Ross and former CEO George Perlegos responsible for a stock options scandal at the semiconductor company. The company said Ross personally benefited from backdated options that were not approved by the Board.

Possibly the most publicized case is that of Greg Reyes in 2007, the former CEO of Brocade Communications Systems Inc. Bloomberg. In a broad government crackdown on options backdating, Reyes was the first chief executive convicted by a jury. He lost his bid to reverse his conviction for backdating employee stock-option grants and hiding the practice from auditors and investors.

He received an 18-month prison sentence and U.S. $15 million fine imposed after his second criminal trial. Brocade investors lost as much as U.S. $197.8 million in 2005 when they sold shares that had fallen in value after the practice was uncovered and the company restated financial results, prosecutors said in court filings.

## Intangible Assets

### *History of Standard*

| | |
|---|---|
| January 1, 1980 | IAS 9 (1978) Accounting for Research and Development Activities issued<br>IAS 9 Accounting for Research and Development Activities effective |
| January 1, 1995 | IAS 9 (1993) Research and Development Costs effective |
| July 1, 1998 | IAS 38 Intangible Assets<br>IAS 38 Intangible Assets effective |
| March 31, 2004 | Amendments |

| January 1, 2009 | Amendments |
|---|---|
| July 1, 2009 | Amendments |
| July 1, 2014 | Amendments |
| January 1, 2016 | Amendments |

What did Facebook get for its money? Certainly not an extensive range of buildings, land, machinery, and other assets you can see and touch. What it paid for was upward of 450 million users.

> In 2014, Facebook bought WhatsApp for U.S. $19 billion in cash and stock. WhatsApp has been in operation for approximately 5 years and had just over 50 employees.

Increasingly, companies have found that their most important assets for generating future benefits are not material assets such as buildings and machinery, but assets that have no physical substance. For an intangible asset to be recognized it must be (a) identifiable and (b) reliably measured. This means that the asset must be capable of being separated from the rest of the company and can be sold, licensed, rented, or exchanged either individually or together with a related item. The intangible asset can also be identifiable because it arises from contractual or legal rights, even if those rights are not separable from the business.

Recognizing and measuring the intangible asset will depend on how it has been identified. Some intangible assets will have been purchased by the company from another entity. The recognition is evident through the purchase and the measurement of the asset is by the price paid.

Some intangibles can be internally generated, in other words, the company has developed the intangible asset itself. For example, a food company may have developed a new slimming food that resulted in a patent, or a company may have developed a special kind of software for controlling its operations that led to increased efficiency.

### *The Problem of Goodwill*

One intangible asset in particular where it has been problematic to agree with the correct accounting treatment is goodwill. This is a term that is difficult to define and somewhat easier to explain through an example.

Consider the case of a very successful company that has built up a strong customer base, designed a range of quality products, and trained a good workforce. The company has gained an excellent reputation; this reputation, however valuable, will not appear anywhere on the financial statements of the company.

Imagine that a very large company acquires a smaller, but highly successful, company. Because the small company is so successful, the large company is willing to pay a high price for it. Let us assume that the price in this case is U.S. $5 million. The purchase is made and the large company calculates the fair value of the tangible assets, such as buildings and machinery, which it has acquired.

The large company calculates the fair value of the net identifiable assets, excluding goodwill, to be U.S. $4 million. As the purchase price was U.S. $5 million, the large company paid an extra U.S. $1 million for its acquisition. This excess represents all those aspects that are not tangible, but has made the smaller company successful, such as its reputation. In accounting, we assume that this payment of U.S. $1 million is for an intangible asset we term goodwill. This asset does not appear on the balance sheet of the smaller company as it was generated internally. However, as the large company has paid for goodwill, it will need to account for it. There are several options of doing so:

1. Write off the cost of goodwill immediately to the income statement. This is not acceptable as U.S. $1 million has been paid for something; if that sum of money has gone out, we need to record what was received in exchange. Acquisitive companies had to convince their investors that they were purchasing something of value that would appear on the balance sheet.
2. Record it on the balance sheet as an intangible asset and leave it there. Companies were mainly in favor of this method as the goodwill was an additional asset on their balance sheet and there were no costs to the income statement. The argument, mainly from standard setters, against this approach is that although the goodwill life may be indefinite, nothing is infinite. The goodwill cannot last forever. This leads us to the third option.

3. The goodwill is placed on the balance sheet as an asset and written off to the income statement over several years in the same way as we do with tangible assets.

In most countries, after considerable experiments with the different methods, option 3 was selected. Not surprisingly, as it was national standard setters deciding for their own country, the periods of write-off time varied considerably, ranging from 5 years to 40 years.

Before 2001, the United States allowed companies to use one of two methods when making an acquisition: the pooling of interests or the purchase method. The first method combined the book value of assets and liabilities of the two companies to create the new balance sheet of the combined companies as if it had always been one. The acquisition price was not disclosed, so there was no goodwill. The second approach, purchase method, did give rise to goodwill and the regulations at that time required goodwill to be written off over 40 years.

In 2001, the FASB issued FAS 142, which, to the dismay of some, removed the pooling of interest option. At the same time, the method of writing off goodwill over 40 years was removed. Instead, it became necessary to review goodwill for impairment, either at the operating level, meaning a business segment, or at a lower organizational level.

Conceptually, there is considerable merit for a policy requiring the write-down of an asset when there has been a significant decline in value. A write-down can provide important information about the future cash flows that a company can generate from using the asset. However, in practice, this process is very subjective. Even if it appears certain that significant impairment of value has occurred, it is often difficult to measure the amount of the required write-down.

The procedure for assessment of impairment must be conducted annually. The computed fair value of a business segment, using the present value of future cash flows, is compared to the carrying value (book value of assets plus goodwill minus liabilities).

Where the book value of the unit exceeds its fair value, no further exercise needs to take place and valuation of goodwill remains unchanged. If, however, the fair value of the reporting unit is lesser than the book value, the goodwill is impaired and the amount of the impairment must be written off.

Under FASB ASC 350, *Intangibles—Goodwill and Other,* the asset of goodwill is tested for impairment at least annually using a two-step process.

With the first step, the reporting unit's fair value, including goodwill, is measured by using an appropriate valuation technique, such as a discounted cash flow method. Fair value is compared to the reporting unit's carrying amount or book value of the goodwill. If the reporting unit's fair value is greater than its carrying amount, the reporting unit's goodwill is not considered to be impaired. If the reporting unit's fair value is less than its carrying amount, then the second step is performed to determine if goodwill is impaired.

In step 2, for all classifications of property, plant, equipment, and intangible assets, the amount of impairment is measured as the excess of the book value of the asset over its fair value. However, unlike for most other assets, the fair value of goodwill cannot be measured directly (market value, present value of associated cash flows, and so on) and so must be implied from the fair value of the reporting unit that acquired the goodwill.

The implied fair value of goodwill is calculated in the same way that goodwill is determined in a business combination. That is, the implied fair value is a residual amount measured by subtracting the fair value of all identifiable net assets from the purchase price. The unit's previously determined fair value is used as the purchase price.

In July 2012, the FASB issued guidance that gives companies the option to perform a qualitative impairment assessment for indefinite-lived intangible assets that may allow them to skip the annual fair-value calculation.

The present U.S. GAAP and international regulations are now very similar with some remaining differences. The international standard IAS 36—Impairment of Assets—has the following principles:

- Acquired goodwill should be recognized.
- Goodwill should be tested for impairment at least annually.
- Goodwill cannot be systematically amortized.
- Goodwill should not be revalued.
- Internally generated goodwill cannot be recognized.

There have been criticisms of the current regulations from users of financial statements who are uncertain about the reliability of the information. Preparers and users also express concern about the cost and complexity of the impairment testing.[16]

There is a considerable amount of work involved in conducting impairment testing for goodwill and the method is questionable as it relies heavily on judgment and estimates. The amounts to be written off can be significant if the company and the industry are experiencing poor economic conditions. For example, in 2012, General Motors Company wrote off goodwill impairment charges of U.S. $27,145 million. The company did not write off any goodwill in the years 2014 to 2016.

We started this section with a question and we will end with one—Is what Facebook bought worth U.S. $19 billion? Because Facebook paid that amount, accountants assume that is the value to appear on the balance sheet. Would other companies have paid that amount? We do not know but several commentators have queried the size of the payment.

If you are an investor in Facebook, we may be confident that they have complied with the regulations. However, you may think that Facebook has overpaid for the intangible assets that will appear on their balance sheet. After all, much of the declared value may represent little more than expectations for the future.

## Leasing

### *History of Standard*

| | |
|---|---|
| January 1, 1999 | IAS 17 Leases effective |
| January 1, 2005 | Revised |
| January 1, 2009 | Amended |
| January 1, 2019 | IFRS 16 Leases effective |

Leasing has become an increasingly important activity in the business world and represents an essential source of funding for companies wishing to acquire or use noncurrent assets. In some taxation jurisdictions, it has been possible to structure agreements so that either, or both, the lessor or lessee enjoy significant taxation benefits.

## Option 1

Barebones could attempt to borrow U.S. $300,000 from the bank. The bank will want repayment of the loan plus interest. If we assume five annual repayments of U.S. $60,000 for the loan and U.S. $12,000 annually for interest:

- The balance sheet will show an asset under machinery of U.S. $300,000 and a liability to the bank of the same amount.
- On payment of each installment, the liability to the bank reduces by U.S. $60,000, and an interest charge goes to the income statement of U.S. $12,000.
- The end of each year brings an annual depreciation charge to the income statement of U.S. $60,000.

There are various methods that can be used to account for a lease. These methods can result in very different entries on the financial statements if there is no accounting standard in place to regulate practices.

Two of these methods can be demonstrated by taking the hypothetical example of Barebones Inc. Assume that the company wishes to buy some machinery with a useful life of 5 years costing U.S. $300,000, but has no cash. It therefore has to seek a method for funding the acquisition; there are two options for the company, assuming that no accounting standards exist.

With Option 1, Barebones will show a large loan on its balance sheet. It may not want to disclose on its financial statements that it has such a loan, as this may be assumed to be a financial weakness.

If you compare Option 2 to Option 1 you will see that the charge to the income statement is the same U.S. $72,000. The big difference is that nothing is shown on the balance sheet although Barebones owes the bank U.S. $300,000.

It is contended that companies may construct agreements to purposely classify leases as operating to avoid putting assets and liabilities on the balance sheet.[17] This practice is made somewhat easier by U.S. GAAP having bright line rules to define the two types of leases.

The original U.S. standard (SFAS 13) defined a capital lease as one under which any one of the following four conditions is met:

1. The present value at the beginning of the lease term of the payments not representing executory costs paid by the lessor equals or exceeds 90 percent of the fair value of the leased asset;
2. The lease transfers ownership of the asset to the lessee by the end of the lease term;
3. The lease contains a bargain purchase price;
4. The lease is equal to 75 percent or more of the estimated economic life of the leased asset.

It does not require much ingenuity to draw up a contract where the percentages fall on the most advantageous side for the company and the information it wishes to disclose.

The original international standard (IAS 17—Accounting for Leases) is principles based. It avoids setting out quantitative thresholds, as is the case in the U.S. standard, but states that the classification of a lease depends on the *substance* of the transaction rather than the *form*. The standard describes situations that would normally lead to a lease being classified as a finance lease, including the following:

- The lease transfers ownership of the asset to the lessee by the end of the lease term;
- The lessee has the option to purchase the asset at a price that is expected to be sufficiently lower than its fair value at the date the option becomes exercisable that, at the inception of the lease, it is reasonably certain that the option will be exercised;
- The lease term is for the major part of the economic life of the asset, even if the title is not transferred;
- At the inception of the lease, the present value of the minimum lease payments amounts to at least substantially all of the fair value of the leased asset; and
- The lease assets are of a specialized nature such that only the lessee can use them without major modifications being made. An example would be where certain equipment is required for certain manufacturing operations unique to the organization.

Under the existing regulations, it was claimed that companies using U.S. standards could structure agreements to avoid the quantitative thresholds and define the lease that best met their purposes.[18] Criticisms on the ethicality of intentionally structuring lease contracts to avoid disclosing leased asset and liability amounts are voiced frequently. There is also the contention that the slippery slope of rule-based *accounting* for synthetic *leases* and special purpose entities led to the *accounting* scandals at Enron and other companies.[19]

Given the substantial differences between the U.S. and International Standards and the claimed abuse of the U.S. standard, it is not surprising that a project was added to the convergence agenda in 2006 to develop a new international accounting standard that addresses the deficiencies in existing regulations for accounting for leases.

The aim of the project was to agree to a single approach to lease accounting. The new standard would ensure the recognition of all assets and liabilities arising under lease contracts in the statement of financial position. The project was lengthy and the two Boards were unable to agree on a joint standard and, finally, issued their own versions.

The IASB's approach covers virtually all leases, other than short term, as finance leases and they will appear as assets on the balance sheet. This includes intangible assets. The FASB's standard only applies to property, plant, and equipment. Whether leases for such assets should appear on the balance sheet depends on a number of criteria that have some resemblance to the original U.S. regulations.

Although it is not presented as a rule, the new FASB lease accounting standard gives guidance as to what constitutes a lease that should appear on the balance sheet. The lease should cover a major part of an asset's life. The standard suggests that one way to determine this is to use the 75 percent test of the original standard FAS 13.

It is impossible to say whether the two standards are sufficiently close to be considered "converged." There are differences, but the main test will be how financial directors and auditors interpret and apply the requirements of the standards.

The classification of a lease depends on whether the lease meets certain criteria.

## Financial Instruments

| | |
|---|---|
| January 1, 2005 | IAS 32 Financial instruments: presentation |
| January 1, 2005 | IAS 39 Financial instruments: recognition and measurement |
| January 1, 2007 | IFRS 7 Financial instruments: disclosures |
| January 1, 2015 | IFRS 9 Financial instruments: 2015 |

The history of financial instruments has had so many changes and amendments that only the effective date of issued standards is given above. This obscures the complexity of the subject and the difficulties in accounting for these transactions.

### *Financial Instruments Explained*

The definition of financial instruments states that there must be a contract and this gives rise to financial assets, financial liabilities, and equity, which appear on a balance sheet. The definition of a financial instrument is also two sided: The contract must always give rise to a financial asset of one party, with a corresponding financial liability or equity instrument of another party.

Financial markets are used by companies to raise finances for their business activities. External financial markets can be considered short term, less than a year, or long term. Short-term financial markets are often called money markets. Long-term financial markets are called capital markets, and include the equity market, the debt market, which includes borrowing from other firms, and the bank market. Multinational companies that used to raise equity capital solely from sources within their own country now look to other countries for potential shareholders; this is known as cross-border financing.

There are several types of risks associated with using financial markets. There is interest rate risk from making investments or taking out loans, or exchange rate risk through international trade. It is impossible to eliminate risk completely. However, companies can attempt to reduce it by hedging the risk.

An example of hedging is as follows: A company knows that it has to purchase supplies of materials in 3 months' time. The materials, such as agricultural crops, may not be ready to be purchased right away, or the company may not wish to hold the materials until they are needed. There is a risk that the price of materials will increase before the end of the 3 months. The company can enter into an agreement now to purchase the goods in 3 months' time, but at the current price. The company avoids the risk of the prices increasing in 3 months' time when it requires the materials. It also loses the opportunity to make a gain if the price decreases in 3 months' time.

Contracts are used for trading in derivatives. These are commonly traded among financial institutions, individual investors, fund managers, corporations, and private companies. The trades are conducted at either a physical location such as an Exchange or remotely in what is termed the over-the-counter market.

The four main types of derivatives are: forward contracts, future contracts, options, and swaps.

### Forward Contract

These contracts are the simplest form of derivatives. One of the parties in a forward contract agrees to buy the underlying asset on a future specified date for a certain specified price. The other party agrees to sell the asset on the agreed date for the agreed price. The price at which the parties agree to transact in the future is called the delivery price. No money changes hands at the time the parties enter into a forward contract. Once forward contracts are agreed upon, they can be traded between investors, typically on the over-the-counter market.

### Futures Contract

A futures contract is very similar to a forward contract. Futures contracts are traded on a variety of commodities, including live cattle, sugar, wool, lumber, copper, gold, and tin. They are also traded on a wide array of financial assets, including stock indexes, currencies, and treasury bonds.

## Options

There are two types of options. In contrast to forward and futures, options give the owner the right, but not the obligation, to transact. The owner, therefore, will only transact if it is profitable to do so. The price at which the parties transact in the future is called the strike price. When the transaction takes place, the owner of the option is said to exercise his option.

## Swaps

A swap is simply an agreement between two parties to exchange cash flows in the future. The agreement defines the dates when the cash flows are exchanged and the manner in which amounts are calculated. Swaps typically lead to cash flow exchanges on several future dates. There are interest rate swaps, where a floating-rate loan is exchanged for a fixed-rate loan by agreeing to pay a fixed payment in return for a variable payment. Similarly, currency swaps can be used to transform borrowings in one currency to borrowings in another currency, by agreeing to make a payment in one currency in return for a payment in another currency.

The global financial crisis of 2007 to 2008 caused considerable panic. Understandably, people wanted to know the cause of the crisis and financial instruments became the focus. The reasons offered for financial instruments being the culprit fell into two main camps. There were those who believed that the complex financial instruments had been used inappropriately. Others, particularly the banks, argued that it was not the financial instruments that were to blame but the way that they had to be accounted for, in other words, the accounting regulations.

The accounting standards were castigated because of the requirement for fair-value accounting. This required valuation of financial assets at their current market value. Thus, fair-value accounting forced companies to write-down financial asset values, destroying equity and weakening banks' lending practices. The defenders of fair-value accounting argued that the method was not the cause of the crisis. They claimed that fair value only revealed the effects of poor decisions.

For the FASB and the IASB, the focus on accounting for financial instruments started in March 2006. The Boards declared their intentions to work together to improve and converge financial reporting standards by issuing a memorandum of understanding (MoU), *A Roadmap for Convergence between IFRS and U.S. GAAP—2006–2008*. As part of the MoU, the Boards worked jointly on a research project to reduce the complexity of the accounting for financial instruments.

Despite the many meetings and issue of documents, the Financial Instruments Project made very slow progress. The main differences in the convergence process have been extracted from a summary by Lin and Fink[20] of several standards and is shown in Table 4.3.

Not only were the two Boards unable to agree on a joint standard, but the failure to do so confirmed that the convergence project was not proving completely successful. In 2012, the FASB and the IASB tried to resolve their differences, but finally decided to develop their own standards. The IASB continued its work in separate phases, whereas the FASB initially decided to issue one exposure draft for comment.

In 2014 the IASB published the complete version of IFRS 9 *Financial Instruments* which replaces most of the guidance in IAS 39. In 2016, the FASB issued Accounting Standards Update 2016-01, *Financial Instruments—Overall: Recognition and Measurement of Financial Assets and Financial Liabilities*. The FASB is continuing its deliberations on hedging.

***Table 4.3 Major differences between U.S. GAAP and IFRS financial instruments—impairment***

| U.S. GAAP | IFRS |
| --- | --- |
| Testing is required only when circumstances change | Testing is required at the end of each reporting period |
| Reversals are not allowed | Reversals are allowed |
| Undiscounted sum of future cash flows is used for measurement | Value-in-use and fair value less costs to sell are used for measurement |

## Conclusion

Standard setting is subject to changes in business activities, political influences, and lobbying by those who support or are opposed to amendments to particular accounting regulations. The FASB and IASB convergence project is directed not only by technical accounting, but also by other influences and we discussed these in the first section of the chapter.

The topics discussed in this chapter demonstrate the complexities and influences on standard setting. They exemplify the successes of convergence but also highlight that convergence may not always be total and differences can remain. The research that has been conducted confirms that the convergence project has narrowed the differences or distance between U.S. GAAP and IFRS. There is also the suggestion that, in doing so, higher-quality standards have been produced, a notion we discussed in Chapter 3.

Although the requirements in the standards may have come closer together, insufficient experience has been gained to assess how the regulations are interpreted in practice. The intended result was that the financial statements of companies in different countries would be comparable, in other words transactions and events would be treated in the same way. Our review of some of the main standards indicates that there are differences between the IASB and the FASB requirements and there will be differences in interpretation.

# CHAPTER 5

# The End and the Beginning

## About This Chapter

In this final chapter we consider the corporate reporting practices that have been taking place because of both technological developments and the interest in nonfinancial information. The final section of the chapter reviews the present relationship between the United States and International Accounting and possible future developments.

The main part of the chapter first considers the developments in the application of technology and its impact on corporate reporting. The Internet has affected all our lives and it has had a major impact on the provision of information by companies. The printed annual report and accounts issued by companies has increased significantly in length. Part of the reason is legislation requiring greater disclosures by companies. Much of this has had a financial basis. But there has also been encouragement for companies to provide nonfinancial information. The opportunity for a company to set up a website for these disclosures has encouraged the growth in both financial and nonfinancial information.

As well as technological developments, there has been a substantial growth in the different types of nonfinancial information that now comprises much of corporate reports. The increasing amount of information has encouraged the linking of the individual types of disclosure to demonstrate their relationships. This is demonstrated in the development of integrated reporting, which removes the distinction between financial and nonfinancial information to provide a comprehensive picture of a company's activities and progress.

There are also many streams of nonfinancial information that come under various headings. We focus on two areas that have increase in perceived importance. One falls under the general title of corporate governance reporting and the other sustainability reporting.

Our final section reviews the position of the Financial Accounting Standards Board (FASB) and international accounting. The convergence project had its successes but did not manage to establish a complete set of international accounting standards. This has not led to the demise of either the FASB or the International Accounting Standards Board (IASB), but leaves open the question of the future of worldwide international accounting.

## Fundamental Barriers

In Chapter 1 we discussed the characteristics in different countries, such as culture, tax, and legislation, and how these presented difficulties in establishing international accounting. Many of those characteristics remain and can delay the adoption of full international accounting by any country. There are also disagreements within countries as to what information should be made publicly available by companies.

The nature of the difficulties of the FASB and the IASB in reaching agreement is evident in documents usually entitled "Conceptual Frameworks." These are intended to spell out the fundamental concepts that underpin the practices of accounting and financial reporting and act as a guide for standard setters in establishing high-quality standards.

Unfortunately, the FASB and the IASB have not been able to agree upon a joint Conceptual Framework. Given the nature of the questions they are trying to resolve, differences of opinion are not unexpected. We have listed below what we consider to be the pertinent questions.

1. *Who* are the users of financial statements?
2. *What* information do they need?
3. *Why* do they need this information?
4. *How* can financial reporting best provide this information?
5. *What* nonfinancial information is required?

The difficulties that exist between the two Boards in answering these questions demonstrate the obstacles of issuing a joint "Conceptual Framework." The Boards, individually, may be able to offer their own answers, but are unable to find a common ground. This problem can be demonstrated by looking at the first question regarding the potential users of financial statements.

The process of identifying the users of corporate financial statements has had a long history. In November 1978, the FASB published *Financial Accounting Concepts No 1.*[1] This publication states that financial reporting should provide information that is useful to present and potential investors, creditors, and other users in making rational investment decisions.

The IASB's views reflect the arguments of an influential 1975 document entitled "The Corporate Report."[2] This proposed that there are seven user groups including investors, employees, prospective employees, and trade unions. To ensure no one group was omitted, the report also included "society at large." This was because of the perceived societal need for information on the economic and other activities of powerful corporate bodies and was possibly an early indicator of the current disclosures, such as corporate governance and sustainability, which we discuss late in this chapter.

The Corporate Report has been viewed as an innovative and enterprising contribution to the discussion of conceptual frameworks. It portrays a much broader vision of social accountability than the investor–creditor focus, which has historically been predominant in the United States.[3] The International Accounting Standards Committee's (IASC) Framework for the Presentation and Preparation of Financial Statements issued in 1989 echoed the sentiments in The Corporate Report. It repeated in its document, IAS 1 Presentation of Financial Statements, first issued in 1997 that:

> The objective of financial statements is to provide information about the financial position, financial performance and cash flows of an entity that is useful to a wide range of users in making economic decisions. Financial statements also show the results of the management's stewardship of the resources entrusted to it.[4]

The last sentence introduces a wider view than a narrow financial focus on financial performance by introducing the term "stewardship." This introduces two models for developing accounting standards. These are often referred to as the decision model and the stewardship model. It is argued that the decision model must provide information that is relevant to the providers of capital, that is, shareholders and lenders. The stewardship model considers that corporate bodies should provide information to a wide range of users who may be interested in the entity's activities. Current employees, suppliers, and customers are good examples of such users.

In 2006, a discussion paper was issued which set out the two Boards' agreed objective of general financial reporting, which was:

> To provide financial information that is useful to present and potential investors, and creditors and others in making investment, credit, and similar resource allocation decisions.[5]

The objective of financial reporting is regarded as decision-making one. The users are identified and so are the types of decision that they make. Such a view was challenged by several respondents who argued that financial reporting has not one, but two objectives: decision making *and* stewardship.

There are various opinions on the meaning of stewardship, but O'Connell[6] reflects the main opinion by contending that

> The contemporary concept of stewardship is synonymous with the notion of accountability to both internal and external parties for the purposes of revealing and evaluating the past actions of both the enterprise and its management and, to some extent, influencing future actions.

It is noticeable that there is no specific reference to financial accounting and the purpose of the information provision is to evaluate actions without narrowing it down to economic performance. This theme was reflected in a discussion paper issued by the UK Accounting Standards Board which issued its own discussion paper (2007). It conducted a detailed review of all the comment letters made to the IASB's discussion paper in 2006, and argued that:

- There is a broad consensus among the majority of the respondents that the stewardship and accountability objective should be a separate objective of financial reporting;

- Stewardship and accountability are linked to the agency theory and are a broader notion than resource allocation as it focuses on both past performance and how the entity is positioned for the future. It should therefore be retained as a separate objective of financial reporting to ensure that there is appropriate emphasis on company performance as a whole and not just on potential future cash flows; and
- Stewardship and accountability have implications for financial reporting, which can be demonstrated by way of examples.

FASB appeared to have some difficulties with the word stewardship but agreed that the wording would be changed to describe what stewardship encapsulates, even if that particular word would not be used. There are currently no signs that the two Boards will meet again with the objective of producing one agreed-upon Conceptual Framework.

If determining who should be the recipients of information, an even more difficult task is defining the legal structure of the organization that should produce financial statements. One must know what comprises the entity to establish the boundaries for producing financial statements. Major companies are listed on stock exchanges. These are usually groups of companies with separate and identifiable companies either wholly owned or partly owned by a holding company.

There are two main theories or perspectives as to what constitutes a group: the proprietary theory and the entity theory. This is critical in determining the scope of the financial information to be disclosed by the entity listed on the stock exchange.

The proprietary theory views the group from the perspective of the proprietors—the major owners of the group. The financial statements of the group should show the total interest owned by the proprietor. In some of the subsidiaries, the holding company will own the major part of the subsidiary, but not 100 percent, and the minor part will be held by other investors. In this instance, the financial statements of the group will show the total interest owned by the holding company either directly or indirectly via the proportional ownership of the subsidiary.

The entity theory perceives the group as a single economic entity. In these circumstances, the financial statements of the group show the total resources managed by the group for the purpose of providing useful information to all of the group's stakeholders, including those with only the minor ownership.

The deliberations by the FASB and the IASB tended to avoid this issue, during the convergence exercise. It is unlikely that they will ever be able to reach agreement on this subject because of the difficulty in defining the role and responsibilities of the shareholder.

An interesting paper[7] on the legal position argues that the popular view of shareholders is that they are the owners of a public company. Accordingly, this is the group entitled to receive financial information on its economic performance. It is questionable whether this view is legally sound. An analysis of nations with publicly listed corporations shows that shareholders are not legally recognized as owners of the company nor of corporate assets. Shareholders, in fact, are owners of a set of freely tradable rights. These entitle them to vote, receive dividends, and claim the residual value of corporate assets.

## The Growth of Annual Reports

The identification and collection of data for annual reporting is a costly business. The requirements and recommendations of any standard setter for various disclosures of information are tempered by the realization that the costs of reporting information must be at least matched by the benefits the users receive. This costs–benefits equation is difficult to calculate for the following reasons:

- The company may prepare the information but the user may suffer the cost in the form of reduced financial returns from the company (e.g., a lower dividend).
- If the needed information is not provided, the user will incur additional costs in obtaining that information by other means.
- Disclosure of financial information that has relevance and faithful representation makes for a more efficient capital market with lower costs for everyone.
- There is no substantial evidence as to the worth of the financial information to the specific users.

*Table 5.1 The growth in U.K. annual reports*

| | 2005 | | 2014 | |
|---|---|---|---|---|
| | Number of pages | % of total | Number of pages | % of total |
| Audit report | 1 | 1 | 4 | 2 |
| Financial statements | 4 | 3 | 5 | 3 |
| Notes to accounts | 39 | 34 | 48 | 29 |
| Other disclosures | 72 | 62 | 111 | 66 |
| TOTAL | 116 | 100 | 168 | 100 |

*Source:* Hussey and Ong (2015).[8]

In concentrating on the financial disclosures, it is easy to forget that for most companies, the Annual Report and Accounts is also a promotional document. For most major companies, possibly less than one-third of the document contains the financial statements. There is also narrative information that the government may require. Table 5.1 shows the growth is a random selection of UK annual reports. The table shows the growth from 2005, when the United Kingdom adopted international accounting to 2014.

The number of pages in the annual report had increased on average by approximately 50 pages. All sections had increased in absolute terms. The growth in the audit report, financial statements, and notes is due to legislation. Other disclosures had increased by 4 percent but this amounted to 52 pages.

To obtain some basic data from the United States we analyzed the reports of five companies chosen at random. We show the results in Table 5.2. Our data show the approximate number of pages for each of the reports.

There are significant differences both in the page lengths of the reports and in the pages attributed to the financial statements and notes. With all five companies the number of pages given to information not required by accounting standards is at least 50% of the entire document.

Many of the present printed annual reports issued by large companies are concerned with products, corporate strategy, successful projects, charitable involvements, and other topics. Several of these disclosures are accompanied by excellent photographs and are printed on high-quality

*Table 5.2 Size of annual reports of U.S. companies*

| Company | Financial statements | Notes to the FS | FS + Notes | Total # of pages |
|---|---|---|---|---|
| Ford | 6 | 53 | 59 | 200 |
| IBM | 6 | 65 | 71 | 164 |
| Amazon | 7 | 30 | 37 | 86 |
| Walmart | 5 | 19 | 24 | 68 |
| Starbucks | 5 | 36 | 41 | 104 |

paper. To a large extent, the total cost of the Annual Report and Accounts is in the control of the companies and is little influenced by the disclosure requirements of accounting standards.

Regardless of what the costs–benefits equation demonstrates, experience has shown that without a form of strong accounting regulations, some companies are tempted to mislead investors. Most countries have therefore established an organization with the specific responsibility of regulating financial information disclosed by companies.

Whether we are considering financial or nonfinancial information, there has been an increase in the amount and types of information disclosed. Corporate reporting, in the broadest sense, has been subject to change in the past and continues to be subject to change. At the global level there is no longer a view of the annual report and accounts as a mainly financial document for the benefit of investors. A company's actions have an impact on society and the environment in which it operates. That has led to discussions on the users of corporate information, the information they want, and the information companies should give.

### *Users of Corporate Reports*

The IASB, possibly influenced by U.S. thinking, has tended to some extent to concentrate on investors and others who require information for making investment decisions. This is not necessarily the view of all regulators. The Financial Reporting Council in the United Kingdom, with the legal authority for corporate disclosures, has a wider brief. In its publications, the term "stakeholder" is used and their different needs examined.

This is not necessarily an indication of the way that the IASB will choose to go but the discussion is being conducted.

### *Information Users Want*

An expansion in the definition of the potential users of corporate reports makes it more difficult to identify a range of information that is manageable. Over recent years there have been several studies that have attempted to establish the information needs of users. It is not possible to draw on these to determine a "package of disclosures" that meets the needs of all users. There is also the reasonable question as to what information a company has and what it is willing to disclose. Undoubtedly, the advent of the internet has made the provision of information much easier for companies.

### *The Information Companies Should Give*

Companies must comply with the legislation of the country in which they were incorporated, the requirements of the stock exchange on which they are listed, and the requirements of the appropriate accounting standards whether these are international standards, as in the EU, or specific to the country, as in the United States.

In the past, companies have frequently chosen to disclose information that it considers meets the interests and concerns of a larger groups than only investors. Environmental disclosures have been made for several years and topics such as governance and sustainability are regularly provided. Some of the disclosures are required by legislation and some are encouraged by "Awards" bestowed by business magazines, firms of accountants, and others.

The impact of companies on the lives of employees, the environment, and society in general became increasingly recognized. The narrowness and weaknesses of financial reporting were the subjects of criticism and this led to the adoption of sustainability reports. It is claimed (Brannen 2007)[9] that these complement financial reports provide information about the environment, social issues, and governance with a future orientation.

Over recent years, the range of disclosures has moved away from only financial to narrative reporting. Some commentators argue that such information can be manipulated and misleading. Others argue that narrative reporting assists all users in understanding a company's activities. Adelberg (1979)[10] researched narrative reporting in the United States. He was referring to narrative reporting but his comments can also apply to the assumptions and estimates that underpin financial reporting.

> Given human behaviour, the placing managers in complete control of the accounting communication process which monitors their performance breeds a situation wherein it is perfectly natural to expect that some managers would obfuscate their failures and underscore their success.

Although there has been a continuing growth in annual reports, there must be some limits to it. It is not feasible for companies to continue to collect and distribute information and there are limits to the amount that users can absorb. The solution to this is for the reporting of information that is material to the needs of the users. There lies the difficulties.

Not only do we not have full agreement on who the users are, we also have little knowledge on the reasons for them requiring corporate information. Even if we restrict our considerations to only financial information, it is difficult to decide what financial information users should receive. Of all the data available to them in the company records, management must determine the information that should be included, excluded, or aggregated with other information.

The concept of materiality appears that it might be helpful in selecting relevant data. If management includes immaterial information, the user may become confused or overwhelmed by the amount of information disclosed.

The International Financial Reporting Standards (IFRSs) issued an Exposure Draft Practice Statement on the application of materiality in 2015, covering the following topics:

- the characteristics of materiality;
- applying materiality when making decisions about presenting and disclosing information;
- deciding whether omissions and misstatements of information are material.

The Exposure Draft adopted a negative definition and argued that information is material if omitting it or misstating it could influence decisions that the primary users of general purpose financial reports make on the basis of financial information about a specific reporting entity. This emphasizes the downside of materiality *IASB Exposure Draft, 2015.*[11]

A contribution to the debate was made by the Financial Reporting Council in the United Kingdom. The FRC pointed out that the Companies Act 2006 does not use the term "material" but the FRC considered that materiality underpins many of the requirements of the Companies Act. It also noted that many of the disclosures made by companies were required by company law or other legislation. In these circumstances, companies were compelled to comply and the question of materiality was not an issue.

The obvious problem is determining what is material to various types of users. The FRC pointed out that there are various separate groups including both retail and institutional investors. All the shareholders have different needs and interests and materiality will differ among the groups.

## Technological Developments

### *Internet Reporting*

The practice of issuing printed annual reports containing only financial information is long gone. The printed document has expanded in size. One reason is the increase in the financial information that companies are obliged to disclose. More importantly is the growth in nonfinancial information that may be required by authoritative bodies in the particular country or may be voluntarily given.

The growth in the provision of both financial and, more importantly, nonfinancial information has been assisted by technology advances, in particular the Internet. In our first section we discuss the use of the Internet by companies and this is followed by sections that discuss Integrated Reporting and Sustainability reporting.

Use of the Internet for corporate reporting has grown at a tremendous pace over the last few years. Various forms of business communication, particularly of a marketing nature, have adopted the technology. It allows companies to communicate text, graphics, sound, and video.

Before 1995, there was very little use of the technology for disseminating financial information. In 1996, the practice developed and then grew rapidly. Research by Craven and Marston (1999)[12] examined the largest 200 companies as listed by market capitalization in the *Financial Times*, January 22, 1998. Table 5.3 shows the types of disclosures.

The study not only identified the nature of the information disclosed but also sought to determine what explained the variations in disclosure by companies. The researchers identified two independent variables: company size and industry type. There were four size variables: turnover, number of employees, total assets employed, and average market value. There were six different industrial categories.

The researchers conducted statistical analysis and we summarize the main findings:

- For each one of the four size variables, companies with a website had a median size about twice as large compared to companies without a website.
- There was positive association between the size variables and the extent of financial disclosure on the Internet.
- There was no relationship between industry type and the extent of financial disclosure on the Internet based on the sample of 206 large companies.

***Table 5.3 Summary of financial reporting on the internet by the sample of top UK companies 1998***

| Financial disclosure | Number | Percentage |
|---|---|---|
| Detailed annual report | 67 | 32.5 |
| Parts or summaries of annual report | 42 | 20.4 |
| Website but no financial information | 44 | 21.3 |
| No website | 52 | 25.2 |
| Unclear/ambiguous | 1 | 0.5 |
| Total | 206 | 100 |

***Table 5.4 Corporate reporting on the internet***

| Disclosure | Number of companies |
|---|---|
| Share information | 25 |
| Financial calendar | 22 |
| Results and presentations | 21 |
| Corporate performance | 20 |
| Investor information | 17 |
| Corporate governance | 14 |
| Regulatory news | 10 |
| Analysts coverage | 10 |
| Annual general meeting | 6 |
| Dividends | 5 |
| Advisors | 3 |
| Debt instruments | 2 |
| Brokerage cover | 1 |
| Credit rating | 1 |
| Directors names | 1 |
| Pension governance | 1 |

*Source:* Hussey and Ong.[13]

The above study was conducted 20 years ago, and the use of the Internet for corporate reporting has expanded substantially. The use of the Internet reporting (IR) has grown in most countries.

As a guide to the types of information we show in Table 5.4 the main disclosures made by 25 UK companies. This analysis is based on the 2014 annual report and accounts and we anticipate that there has been further growth since that time.

Much of the research conducted has examined the disclosures by companies on their web pages. One interesting study sought to ascertain what corporate information Internet users seek (Rowbottom, Allam, and Lymer 2005).[14] They measured online information using activity logs from the webserver as this fulfils user requests for information over the Internet. They gathered data from a UK FTSE 100 company.

The researchers carefully explain the limitations of the methodology and the issues in interpretation of the results. The web log analyses do not provide absolute levels of online information usage. They measure what information is demanded online. They do not indicate whether the information has been used or read. They provide a proxy measure of online IR information usage and are not an appropriate proxy for general IR information usage.

Having given those disclaimers, we summarize some of the findings most relevant to this chapter. We emphasize that this research concentrated on the annual report and accounts. Data on all the other information that users place on their Investors Website were not included.

### The Financial Section of the Annual Report and Accounts

- The most visited financial reporting information is the Profit or Loss Account.
- The Notes to the Accounts and the Balance Sheet come second.
- The Cash Flow Statement and the Statement of Total Recognized Gains and Losses are among the least requested parts of the report.

### The Narrative Section of the Annual Report and Accounts

The most requested information is the Remuneration Report and the statement on compliance with the Combined Code for Corporate Governance.

This research gives some insights as to what information users seek on the Internet. This study is over 10 years old and present activity may have changed. Certainly, the amount and range of information on the websites has increased. As well as providing users with easy access to information, the Internet also allows users to search for more detailed financial information.

The SEC, FASB, and the IASB have all been concerned with the provision of disaggregated information in corporate financial statements. It is considered that this would improve the quality of information and the ease of using it.

There are obvious benefits and costs of providing investors with the ability to use disaggregated information to its fullest. Certainly there are costs to the company in providing disaggregated financial information for users, although the availability of detailed information is enhanced.

From the users' perspective there is the possibility of conducting detailed analysis of corporate financial information but there is also the issue that some users may suffer from technology overload.

The International Integrated Reporting Council (IIRC), whose work we discuss in the next section, has suggested that materiality of information is best determined by adopting the following process:

1. Identify relevant matters based on their ability to affect value creation;
2. Evaluate the importance of relevant matters in terms of their known or potential effect on value creation;
3. Prioritize the matters based on their relative importance;
4. Determine the information to disclose about material matters.

Although the recommendations are clear, we consider that these and other suggestions cannot be applied. We have a range of users and a mass of information. What might be relevant to one group of users may be of no interest to a different group.

Although limited to the disclosure of corporate governance, a proposal by Eccles and Youmans[15] has some guidance for specific disclosures. They suggest that the Board issue each year a one-page "Statement of Significant Audiences and Materiality." The document is intended for management, providers of financial capital, and all other stakeholders the board believes to be critical to the long-run profitability and survival of the corporation.

The document would show the board's understanding of its audiences and its decisions to invest resources and management attention over a future time frame. The authors argue that the document would show the Board's vision of the role of the corporation in society, and the financial and nonfinancial (e.g., environmental, social, and governance) foundation for the company's corporate reporting.

Such a document may well be valuable as a communication by the Board with all its users and reveal the Board's vision of the future. However, it does not explain or attempt to assess the materiality of all the financial and nonfinancial information that a company has to disclose.

A further development in the technology of corporate reporting is Extensible Business Reporting Language (XBRL). The system allows printed financial statements to be converted into a computer-readable format. This makes it far easier for investors and others conducting a financial analysis to do so much more easily.

The IFRS is a strong supporter of this use of technology and in the United States large public companies have had to file financial statements using XBRL since 2009 with smaller issues using the technology starting to file between 2009 and 2011.

## New Disclosures

In this section we consider developments that are significant and do not involve the IASB, but are influential and international. Such developments may be introduced by national governments, encouraged by various groups, or be voluntarily undertaken by companies. We have selected three topics, although there are several initiatives in disclosure taking place.

### *Integrated Reporting*

Originally annual reports focused solely on financial information. Over the years the disclosures have grown so that there are usually at least three separate sections. Financial statements are a significant part but there may also be a Management Discussion and Analysis, Strategic Reports, Sustainability data Governance disclosures, Corporate governance, and other information that is not specifically financial. The 2007/2008 economic crisis revealed that financial reporting by itself does not provide sufficient information on short-term and long-term existence of a company.

Commentators have argued that companies should attempt to make the relationships between these different sections stronger. There are criticisms that too much of the document is "boiler plate" material, that is, it is merely repeated year after year. The notes to the financial statements frequently contain text that is merely copied direct from the accounting standards. The emphasis too often is on merely disclosure and not explanation. It would be unfair to criticize all companies with these practices but there has been enough concern for proposals to revise substantially corporate reports.

These developments have led to what is referred to as integrated reporting and this is promoted by the IIRC. This is a global coalition of regulators, investors, companies, standard setters, the accounting profession, and nongovernment organizations.

The coalition is promoting communication about value creation as the next step in the evolution of corporate reporting. The first few words of its website states that Integrated Reporting has been created to "enhance accountability, stewardship and trust." Integrated reporting is now a leading practice in Japan and is part of the stock exchange listing rules in South Africa and Brazil.

In February 2013, the IASB and the IIRC agreed that the two organizations would deepen their cooperation on the IIRC's work to develop an integrated corporate reporting framework.

The IIRC's Framework, dated December 2013, provides companies with a starting point for driving thinking and reporting in an integrated way. The Framework has the following four sections:

- Using the framework
- Fundamental concepts
- Guiding principles
- Content elements

An integrated report is far broader than the present financial statements. It contains details of how an organization's strategy, governance, performance, and prospects lead to the creation of value over the short, medium, and long term. Integrated reports have the primary audience as the providers of financial capital but contain information of interest to a wide range of stakeholders.

The fundamental concepts of integrated reporting are concerned with the various capitals that the organization uses and affects, the organization's business model, and the creation of value over time. In using the word capital, the IIRC departs from the way that we use the term in financial accounting. Capital usually refers to equity, but the Integrated Reporting Model has identified six different capital inputs.

Not all organizations have the same capitals or the same balance. In some organizations, the relationships with some of the capitals are so minor that they are not disclosed in the integrated report. This information can provide an input into the analysis of the financial statements that the user is making.

We list below the six inputs with a brief summary of their nature.

*Financial Capital* – Funds obtained through financing, such as debt equity or grants, or generated through operations or investment

*Manufacturing Capital* – Assets used for producing goods or providing services

*Intellectual Capital* – Knowledge-based intangibles including intellectual property and organizational capital

*Human Capital* – People's competencies, capabilities, and experience. Their motivations to innovate and their support for the organization's values

*Social and Relationship Capital* – The institutions and the relationships within and between communities, groups of stakeholders, and other networks

*Natural Capital* – All renewable and nonrenewable environmental resources and processes that provide goods or services that support the past, current, or future prosperity of an organization

The IIRC has offered guiding principles and these are:

A) Strategic focus and future orientation
B) Connectivity of information
C) Stakeholder relationships
D) Materiality
E) Conciseness
F) Reliability and completeness
G) Consistency and comparability

We would add to this that the major firms of accountants are beginning to issue reports extolling the benefits of integrated reporting. It is too early to know whether the proposals will be successful but the actions by the EU and the proposals by the IIRC show where corporate reporting is moving: and accountants are fully involved in these developments.

In 2017, Richard Howitt was appointed as a new head of the IIRC. He has taken on the task of building support for integrated reporting in the United States. He is quoted[16] as saying at a meeting in New York that progress on integrated reporting is increasing and "We want to make more in the United States." There are some excellent examples of integrated reporting in the United States and the indications are that the practice is likely to spread to many companies.

### *Corporate Governance*

Over the years, companies have been growing larger and their activities more pervasive. There have been concerns about the environmental damage caused by some industrial practices, work conditions, and product safety. The response in the United Kingdom provides an example but it is not only that country that has taken steps to satisfy public disquiet.

The Financial Reporting Council in the United Kingdom has published the Combined Code on Corporate Governance that applies to all companies with a premium listing of equity shares on the London Stock Exchange even if the company was not incorporated in the United Kingdom. It is not a list of rules but offers a guide to what may be considered good practice. If a company is unable to comply with the Code it must explain the reasons to shareholders. The company's Board of Directors is responsible for managing the business and reporting to shareholders on their stewardship of the company.

There are five main principles in the Code with several supporting principles.

*Leadership* – There should be an effective board responsible for the company's success.

*Effectiveness* – The board should have the requisite balance of skills, experience, and knowledge of the company.

*Accountability* – The board is responsible for deciding the application of corporate reporting, risk management, and internal control principles.

*Remuneration* – No director can set his or her own remuneration.

*Shareholders* – The board is responsible for ensuring that there is a satisfactory dialogue with shareholders with a clear understanding of objectives.

Strong corporate governance is supported by a Stewardship Code. This states that directors do not have the ultimate responsibility for all of a company's decisions. The directors are responsible to the owners who are deemed to be the shareholders and these are mainly considered to be institutional investors. Under the Code the institutional investors have numerous responsibilities that should include their public announcement on their policy on satisfying their stewardship and they should report periodically on their stewardship and voting activities.

### *Sustainability Reporting*

Such terms as sustainability reporting, social responsibility reporting, and environmental reporting have been appearing in the annual reports of companies for several years. Whether regulated or voluntary such disclosures resolve the possible conflict between economic growth and the concerns of society. There is frequently an overlapping or merging of the terms used, but in this section we will concentrate on sustainability.

Sustainability has been defined as "the generation, analysis and use of monetarized environmental and socially related information in order to improve corporate environmental, social and economic performance" (Bent and Richardson 2003[17]). It meets the needs of present society without impairing the ability of future generations to meet their own needs.

There are different approaches to the pursuit of sustainability reporting. In Australia, the legal requirements come under the Corporations Act 2001. The main requirements are that companies include details of breaches of environmental laws. Also providers of financial products with an investment component should disclose such breaches.

Many countries have not pursued a regulatory route and in the United States there is a Sustainability Accounting Standards Board (SASB). It was established in 2011and is an independent, private-sector organization with the objective of developing sustainability accounting standards that assist public corporations in disclosing material decision—useful information to investors. Both US companies and foreign public companies can use the standard.

The approach of the SASB is to develop standards for specific industries and address sustainability issues in that industry. To better categorize companies that share similar resource intensity, as well as sustainability risks and opportunities, the Board has created the Sustainable Industry Classification System.

The standards the SASB issues have the following characteristics:

- *Objectivity*—Criteria should be free from bias.
- *Measurability*—Criteria should permit reasonably consistent measurements, qualitative or quantitative, of subject matter.
- *Completeness*—Criteria should be sufficiently complete so that those relevant factors that would alter a conclusion about subject matter are not omitted.
- *Relevance*—Criteria should be relevant to the subject matter.

There are numerous governments and other organizations offering encouragement and advice on sustainability reporting. We can assume that sustainability is an international practice and the IASB has no direct involvement. Due to the different use of terms it is impossible to determine the extent and value of what can be identified as sustainability reporting at the international level. However, a survey (KPMG 2011)[18] found that 95% of the 250 largest companies in the world were reporting on corporate responsibility.

## The U.S. and International Accounting

As standard setters, the FASB cannot claim unique resources or knowledge that are not enjoyed by other standard setters. It is well resourced and has extremely knowledgeable people working for it—as do other organizations, but possibly with not so much resourcing. However, it can be argued that other countries have followed U.S. Generally Accepted Accounting Principles (GAAP) for reasons other than the excellence of the standards.

First, there was the requirement for many years that foreign companies wishing to list in the United States had to comply with U.S. GAAP. Although that requirement has changed, several foreign companies already listed have continued to comply rather than the effort of changing their accounting procedures to comply with IFRSs.

Second, the size of the U.S. capital markets has historically attracted companies and investors. That position has weakened during some periods. This observation is not meant to minimize the strength of the U.S. markets, but to note that the international competition is becoming stronger.

Third, the United States has many international companies and extensive business involvement with several countries. The U.S. GAAP had, therefore, become the lingua franca of accounting in some regimes. What the United States has been able to offer, which is missing in some countries, is strong compliance and enforcement procedures. Nearly every research study that examines the application of IFRS emphasizes that the extent of compliance is not due to the defects of the standards but the lack of rigorous enforcement of the standards in some jurisdictions. Countries can copy the requirements of U.S. GAAP or IFRS, but this does not mean that domestic financial statements are truly convergent with IFRS.

A study[19] of four countries identified three dominant factors that are barriers to accounting convergence. These are:

1. The nature of business ownership and the financial system
2. Culture
3. The level of accounting education and the experience of professional accountants

We discussed such factors in Chapter 1, but the above findings highlight the fact that it is not necessarily the regulations set by the standard setters that are the issue, but the environment in which they are being applied. As long as the standards are considered to be of high quality, it does not matter whether the FASB or the IASB sets them; the crucial ingredient is the structure within a country that ensures organizational compliance.

Given the failure of U.S. GAAP and IFRS to converge, the question is what the next step is. It is evident that the IASB has decided to follow its own path. This does not mean the exclusion of U.S. involvement but convergence is no longer an aim. The United States has an international presence and can influence the further development of international corporate reporting, both financial and nonfinancial.

The IFRS Foundation has established an Accounting Standards Advisory Forum to provide an advisory mechanism. This is a way for members of the forum to constructively contribute toward the achievement of the IASB's goal of developing globally accepted, high-quality accounting standards. The following were elected to membership in 2013.

- South African Financial Reporting Standards Council, supported by the Pan African Federation of Accountants (PAFA)
- Group of Latin American Standard Setters (GLASS), represented by the Brazilian Committee of Accounting Pronouncements
- Canadian Accounting Standards Board
- U.S. FASB
- Accounting Standards Board of Japan (ASBJ)
- Australian Accounting Standards Board (AASB)
- Chinese Accounting Standards Committee (CASC)
- Asia Oceania Standard Setters Group (AOSSG), represented by the Hong Kong Institute of Certified Public Accountants (HKICPA)
- Accounting Standards Committee of Germany (ASCG)
- European Financial Reporting Advisory Group (EFRAG)
- Spanish Accounting and Auditing Institute
- United Kingdom Financial Reporting Council (FRC)

The United States still has an international role, although the convergence project is definitely at an end. The present indications are that the forum will concentrate on financial reporting. That leaves the topic of nonfinancial disclosures without authoritative guidance. It is possible that the United States will become a major player in that arena. It has developed an expertise in sustainability reporting and some companies have included nonfinancial disclosures. However, the reasons for the final failure of the convergence project may also hamper any future international developments in narrative reporting.

## Conclusion

The search for convergence has ended, and the United States has decided to follow its own course. It will still retain an international accounting presence, but the emphasis will be on satisfying the needs of its domestic market.

In this final chapter, we have examined two fundamental issues that have always been present and have never been resolved: the rules-based and principles-based approaches and their influence on the development of a conceptual framework. The United States has been inclined to develop standards where the rules that companies should follow when preparing financial statements are very clear. The IASB has tended to issue standards that contain the general principles that accountants should apply when preparing financial statements.

No matter how we describe it and attempt to make accommodations, the U.S. approach is rules based and the IASB principles based. These approaches are mutually exclusive. Although the early signs of a joint Conceptual Framework were promising, as several years passed, any hopes of agreement faded. Some would even argue that the two Boards were unable to produce an agreed list of who the users of financial statements are.

In looking at the reasons for the demise of the convergence project, it should not be forgotten that many achievements were also made. In Chapter 3 we discussed the influence of the convergence project on U.S. accounting regulations. There have also been changes in international standards. Because of the work of the two Boards, accounting regulations have been greatly improved. Whether they are all "high-quality" standards has not been determined.

It would seem that the future of U.S. accounting regulations will not be convergence but some form of compromise with international accounting standards. Our opinion is that it will be the compromise option, with the United States having a strong international influence but maintaining firm control of its own standard-setting structure and processes.

However, the future of the IASB is unclear. The United Kingdom has stated that it will leave the European Union. Currently, it is the EU that endorses international standards and all countries that are members of the EU must follow these standards. If the United Kingdom is no longer a member of the EU then it must decide how it will continue its standard-setting process. The only way would appear that it must set up its own regulatory framework. It is not beyond the boundaries of probability that either the EU or the United Kingdom would decide not to endorse a standard. If this were to happen it would weaken the IASB.

However, the growth in the provision of nonfinancial information continues, as does the use of technology. It could be that these movements will bring about a measure of convergence in the annual report and accounts but still leave flexibility in disclosures for companies to satisfy the information needs of its particular users of corporate reports.

In this final chapter, we have discussed various scenarios for the future. It is apparent that the United States will not have the influence it previously had on the accounting world, but it still intends to remain active at the international level. The future may be uncertain, but we leave our concluding words to R. Hertz,[20] a former Chair of FASB:

> Geo-economic and geo-political forces, coupled with the growing acceptance of IFRS around the world as the recognized set of international accounting standards, will continue to exert pressure on the United States (and other countries) to either adopt IFRS or to continue to move their standards closer to IFRS.

# Notes

## Chapter 1

1. Miller (1965).
2. Securities and Exchange Commission (SEC) (2004).
3. SEC (2003).
4. SEC (2011).
5. SEC (2016).
6. Mueller (1967); Frank (1979); Nair and Frank (1980); Nobes (1983).
7. Nobes (1983).
8. Nobes (2011).
9. Hofstede (1980).
10. Gray (1980).
11. Galbraith (2009).
12. SEC (2016).
13. SEC (2014).
14. PricewaterhouseCoopers LLP (2009).

## Chapter 2

1. Ramanna and Sletten (2009).
2. Johnson and Hicks (2012).
3. Asare and Wright (2012).
4. Narktabtee and Patpanichchot (2011).
5. Daske, Hail, Leuz, and Verdi (2008).
6. Kim, Tsui, and Yi (2011).
7. http://www.iasplus.com/en/resources/ifrs-topics/use-of-ifrs
8. Walker (1987 p. 269).
9. George, Ferguson, and Spear (2011).
10. Richardson (2011, pp. 110—111).
11. CFERF (2013).
12. ICAEW (2012).
13. Zeff and Nobes (2010).
14. Steinback and Tan (2014).
15. Miao (2016).
16. Hou, Jin, and Wang (2014).

17. Sharma, Joshi, and Kansal (2017).
18. Uzma (2016).
19. Tsunogaya, Hellman, and Scagnelli (2015).
20. Tsunogaya (2016).
21. Ozu, Nakamura, Nagata, and Gray (2017).

## Chapter 3

1. Kirsch (2012).
2. Hertz and Petrone (2005).
3. Financial Accounting Standards Board (FASB) (1999, p. 1).
4. Street, Gray, and Bryant (1999).
5. Street (2002, p. 89).
6. Kirsch (2012, p. 47).
7. Hail, Leuz, and Wysocki (2010).
8. Gornik, Tomaszewski, and Showerman (2010, p. 59).
9. Chakravarty (2009).
10. Standard and Poor (2004, 2009).
11. GBFI. This is money (2014).
12. Yallapragada (2012).
13. Gornik-Tomaszewski and Showerman (2010).
14. Canadian Financial Executives Research Foundation (2013, p. 3).
15. Kaya and Pillhofer (2013).
16. American Accounting Association Financial Reporting Policy Committee (AAA FRC) (2010, p. 118).
17. Miller and Becker (2010).
18. Khurana and Michas (2011).
19. Street (2011).
20. SEC (2007).
21. AAA FRC (2010).
22. SEC (2009).
23. Institute of Chartered Accountants in England and Wales (2012).
24. Perrin (2013).
25. Miller and Bahnson (2013).
26. SEC (2000).
27. Barth et al. (2012).
28. White (2017).
29. Nelson (2003).
30. Collins, Pasewark, and Riley (2012).
31. McGregor (1996).
32. Financial Reporting Council (FRC) (2005).

33. FRC (2012).
34. Evans (2003).
35. Alexander and Jermakowicz (2006).
36. FASB website (Comparability in International Accounting Standards—An Overview).

## Chapter 4

1. Holzmann and Hunter (2015).
2. PwC and Financial Executives Research Foundation (FERF) (2016).
3. Rutledge, Karim, and Kim (2016).
4. Du, Alford and Smith (2016).
5. Miller et al. (n.d.).
6. Harris, Kinkela, Stahlin, and Arnold (2014).
7. ASA (n.d.).
8. Hughen, Livingstone, and Upton (2011).
9. Frankel and Hsu (2016).
10. Feldman (2002).
11. Cudd and Smalt (2005).
12. Farber, Johnson, and Petroni (2007).
13. Financial Accounting Standards Board (2004).
14. Persons (2012).
15. Swanton (2007).
16. Pounder (2014).
17. Fleming and Bosco (2006).
18. Henry, Lin, and Yang (2009).
19. Frecka (2008).
20. Lin and Fink (2014).

## Chapter 5

1. FASB (1978).
2. Accounting Standards Steering Committee (1975).
3. Zeff (2013).
4. International Accounting Standards Committee (1997).
5. International Accounting Standards Board (2006).
6. O'Connell (2007).
7. Eccles and Youmans (2016).
8. Hussey and Ong (2015).

9. Brannen (2007).
10. Adelburg (1979).
11. IASB Exposure Draft (2015).
12. Craven and Marston (1999).
13. Hussey and Ong (2017).
14. Rowbottom, Allam, and Lymer (2005).
15. Eccles and Youmans (2016).
16. Cohn (2017).
17. Bent and Richardson (2003).
18. KPMG (2011).
19. Chand, Patel, and Day (2008).
20. Hertz (2013).

# References

AAA FRC (American Accounting Association Financial Reporting Policy Committee). 2010. "Response to the SEC's Proposed Rule—Roadmap for the Potential Use of Financial Statements Prepared in Accordance with International Financial Reporting Standards (IFRS) by U.S. Issuers." *Accounting Horizons* 24, no. 1, pp. 117–128.

Accounting Standards Steering Committee. 1975. *The Corporate Report.* London.

Adelberg, A.H. 1979. "Narrative Disclosures Contained in Financial Reports: Means of Communication or Manipulation?" *Accounting and Business Research* 9, pp. 179–190.

Alexander, D., and E. Jermakowicz. 2006. "A True and Fair View of the Principles/Rules Debate." *Abacus* 42, no. 2, pp. 132–164.

Asare, S.K., and A.M. Wright. 2012. "Investors', Auditors', and Lenders' Understanding of the Message Conveyed by the Standard Audit Report on the Financial Statements." *Accounting Horizons* 26, no. 2, pp. 193–217.

Barth, M.E., W.R. Landsman, M. Lang, and C. Williams. 2012. "Are IFRS- based and US GAAP-based Accounting Amounts Comparable." *Journal of Accounting and Economics* 54, pp. 68–93.

Bent, D. and Richardon, J. 2003. "The Sigma Guidelines: Toolkit for the Future." *British Institute of Management.*

Brannen, L. 2007. "The Sustainability Reporting Evolution." *Business Finance* 13, no. 2, p. 4.

Canadian Financial Executives Research Foundation. 2013. *The Cost of IFRS Transition in Canada.* Canadian Financial Executives Research Foundation, Canada.

Chakravarty, M. August, 2009. "The Global Shift in Market Capitalization." http://www.livemint.com/Money/qg5FD1W5zJYLw20VxUsyxM/The-global-shift-in-market-capitalization.html

Chand, P., C. Patel, and R. Day. July, 2008. "Factors Causing Differences in the Financial Reporting Practices in Selected South Pacific Countries in the Post Convergence Period." *Asian Academy of Management Journal* 13, no. 2, pp. 111–129.

Collins, D.L., W.R. Pasewark, and M.E. Riley. 2012. "Financial Reporting Outcomes under Rules-Based and Principles-Based Accounting Standards." *Accounting Horizons* 26, no. 4, pp. 681–705.

Craven, B.M. and Marston, C.L. 1999. "Financial Reporting on the Internet by Leading U.K. Companies." *European Accounting Review* 8, no. 2, pp. 321–333.

Cudd, A.E., and S.W. Smalt. August, 2005. "Accounting for Stock Options: The Debate Continues." *Journal of Accounting and Finance Research* 13, no. 3, pp. 163–183.

Daske, H., L. Hail C. Leuz, and V. Rodrigo. December 2008. "Mandatory IFRS Reporting Around the World: Early Evidence on the Economic Consequences." *Journal of Accounting Research* 46, no. 5, pp. 1085–1142.

Du, N., R. Alford and P. Smith. 2016. "Do GAAP And IFRS Differ In Collectiblity Judgments Related To Revenue Recognition?" *Journal of Applied Business Research* 32, no. 6, pp. 1675–1686.

Eccles, R.G. and T. Youmans. Spring, 2016. "Materiality in Corporate Governance: The Statement of Significant Audiences and Materiality" *Journal of Applied Corporate Finance* 28, no. 2, pp. 39–46.

Evans, L. 2003. "The True and Fair View and the "Fair" Presentation Override of IAS 1." *Accounting and Business Research* 33, no. 4, pp. 25–37.

Farber, D.B., M.F. Johnson, and K.R. Petroni. March, 2007. "Congressional Intervention in the Standard-Setting Process: An Analysis of the Stock Option Accounting Reform Act of 2004." *Accounting Horizons* 21, no. 1, pp. 1–22.

Feldman, A. September, 2002. "The Real Accounting Scandal." *Money* 31, no. 9, pp. 48–50.

FASB. 1978. *Financial Accounting Concepts No 1: Objectives of Financial Reporting by Business Enterprises.* Norwalk, CT: FASB. http://www.fasb.org/jsp/FASB/Page/SectionPage&cid=1176156245663

FASB. 1999. *International Accounting Standard Setting: A Vision for the Future.* Norwalk, CT: FASB. http://www.fasb.org/jsp/FASB/Page/SectionPage&cid=1176156245663

FASB. December, 2004. FASB Issues Final Statement on Accounting for Share-Based Payments, http://www.iasplus.com/en/binary/usa/0412fasbprfas123r.pdf

FRC (Financial Reporting Council). 2005. *The Implications of New Accounting and Auditing Standards For the True and Fair View.* London: FRC.

FRC. 2012. *FRS100 Application of Financial Reporting requirements.* London.

Fleming, M., and W. Bosco. July, 2006. "Lease Accounting: Are Current Rules as Bad as Some Say?" *Financial Executive* 23, no. 6, pp. 16–17.

Frank, W.G. Autumn, 1979. "An Empirical Analysis of International Accounting Principles." *Journal of Accounting Research* 17, no. 2, pp. 593–605.

Frankel, M and P. Hsu. 2016. "Repeal of LIFO: Analysis Based on Industry Data," *SSRN* 18, no. 6, pp. 11–19.

Frecka, T. June, 2008. "Ethical Issues in Financial Reporting: Is International Structuring of Lease Contracts to Avoid Capitalization Unethical?" *Journal of Business Ethics* 80, no. 1, pp. 45–59.

Galbraith, K. 2009. *The Great Crash 1929.* Reprint ed. Mariner Books.

Gornik-Tomaszewski, S., and S. Showerman. 2010. "IFRS in the United States: Challenges and Opportunities." *Review of Business* 30, no. 2, pp. 59–70.

Gray, S.J. Spring, 1980. "The Impact of International Accounting Differences from a Security Analysis Perspective: Some European Evidence." *Journal of Accounting Research* 18, no. 1, pp. 64–76.

Hail, L., C. Leuz, and P. Wysocki. 2010a. "Global Accounting Convergence and the Potential Adoption of IFRS by the U.S. (Part I): Conceptual Underpinnings and Economic Analysis." *Accounting Horizons* 24, no. 3, pp. 355–394.

Harris, P., K. Kinkela, W. Stahlin, and L.W. Arnold. 2014. "The Present and Future Outlook of the Last in First Out Inventory Methods." *Global Conference on Business and Finance Proceedings* 9, no. 1, pp. 183–187.

Henry, E., S. Lin, and Y. Yang. 2009. "The European-U.S. 'GAAP Gap': IFRS to U.S. GAAP Form 20-F Reconciliations." *Accounting Horizons* 23, no. 2, pp. 121–150.

Hertz, R and K.R. Petrone. Spring, 2005. "International Convergence of Accounting Standards: Perspectives from the FASB on Challenges and Opportunities". *Northwestern Journal of International Law and Business* 25, no. 3, pp 631–659.

Hertz, R. September, 2013. "Convergence's End Will Bring New Opportunities." *Compliance Weekly*, pp. 38–40.

Hofstede, G.H. 1980. *Culture's Consequences: International Differences in Work Related Values.* Beverly Hills, CA: Sage Publications.

Holzmann, O. J. and P. Munter. 2015. "Challenges in Achieving Convergence Between U.S. GAAP and IFRS—The Case of the Revenue Recognition Standard." *Journal of Corporate Accounting & Finance*, pp. 101–106.

Hou Q., Q. Jin, and L. Wang. 2014. "Mandatory IFRS adoption and executive compensation: Evidence from China." *China Journal of Accounting Research* 7, no. 1, pp. 9–29.

Hughen, L., J.R. Livingstone, and D. Upton. April, 2011. "Switching from LIFO Strategies for Change." *CPA Journal*, pp. 26–29.

Hussey, R. and A. Ong. October, 2015. "The expanding waistline of annual reports and accounts." *Accounting and Business Magazine.*

Hussey, R. and A. Ong. 2017. *Corporate Financial Reporting.* UK: Palgrave.

IASC (International Accounting Standards Committee). 1997. *IAS 1 Framework for the Preparation and Presentation of Financial Statements.* London: IASC.

IASB (International Accounting Standards Board). 2006. *The Conceptual Framework for Financial Reporting.* London: IASB.

ICAEW (Institute of Chartered Accountants in England and Wales). 2012. *The Future of Financial Reporting.* London: ICAEW.

Kirsch R.J. June, 2012. "The Evolution of the Relationship between the US Financial Accounting Standards Board and the International Accounting Standards Setters 1973–2008." *Accounting Historians Journal* 39, no. 1, pp. 1–51.

KPMG. 2011. Survey of Corporate Responsibility Reporting. http://www.kpmg.com/crreporting

Miller, N.C. 1965. *The Great Salad Oil Swindle.* New York, NY: Penguin.

Miller, W. and D. Becker. August, 2010. "Why are Accounting Professors Hesitant to Implement IFRS?" *CPA Journal* 80, no. 8, pp. 63–67.

Mueller, G.G. 1967. *International Accounting.* New York, NY: Macmillan.

Nair, R.D., and W.G. Frank. July, 1980. "The Impact of Disclosure and Measurement Practices on International Accounting Classification." *Accounting Review* 55, pp. 426–450.

Nelson, M. March, 2003. "Behavioral Evidence on the Effects of Principles and Rules Based Standards." *Accounting Horizons* 17, no. 1, pp. 91–104.

Nobes, C.W. Spring 1983. "A Judgmental International Classification of Financial Reporting Practices." *Journal of Business, Finance and Accounting* 10, no. 1, pp. 1–19.

O'Connell, V. 2007. "Reflections on Stewardship Reporting." *Accounting Horizons* 21, no. 2, pp. 215–222.

Ozu, C., M. Nakamura, K. Nagata, and S. Gray. 2017. "Transitioning to IFRS in Japan: Corporate Perceptions of Costs and Benefits." *Australian Accounting Review*, pp. 1–10.

Perrin, S. 2013. Hoogervorst reaches out, AB International Edition, pp. 30–31.

Persons, O.S. Spring, 2012. "Stock Option and Cash Compensation of Independent Directors and Likelihood of Fraudulent Financial Reporting." *Journal of Business & Economic Studies* 18, no. 1, pp. 54–74.

Pounder, B. 2014. "Accounting for Goodwill: Back to the Good Old Days." pp. 15–16.

PricewaterhouseCoopers. 2009. *FASB Accounting Standards Quick Reference Guide.* PricewaterhouseCoopers.

PwC and Financial Executives Research Foundation (FERF). 2016. *Revenue Recognition Survey.*

Ramanna, K., and E. Sletten. 2009. "Why do Countries Adopt International Financial Reporting Standards?" Harvard Business School Accounting & Management Unit Working Paper No. 09-102. Harvard Business School.

Richardson, A.J. 2011. "Regulatory Competition in Accounting. A History of the Accounting Standards Authority of Canada." *Accounting History Review* 21, no. 1, pp. 95–114.

Rowbottom, N., Allam, A., and Lymer, A. 2005. "An Exploration for the Potential of Studying the Usage of Investor Relations Information Through the Analysis of Web Sercer Logs" *International Journal of Accounting Information Systems* 6, pp. 31–53.

Rutledge, R., K. Karim, and T. Kim. 2016. "The FASB's and IASB's New Revenue Recognition Standard: What Will Be the Effects on Earnings

Quality," *Journal of Corporate Accounting and Finance*. pp. 43–8. doi:10.1002/jcaf.22188.

SEC. 2000. RELEASE NOS. 33-7801, 34-42430; INTERNATIONAL SERIES NO. 1215, www.sec.gov/rules/concept/34-42430.htm

SEC. 2003. *Six Former Senior Executives of Xerox Settle SEC Enforcement Action Charging Them with Fraud; Executives Agree to Pay Over $22 million in Penalties, Disgorgement and Interest*. Washington, DC: SEC.

SEC. 2004. *Bristol-Myers Squibb Company Agrees to Pay $150 million to Settle Fraud Charges*. Washington, DC: SEC.

SEC. 2007a. *Roadmap for the Potential Use of Financial Statements Prepared in Accordance with International Financial Reporting Standards (IFRS) by U.S. Issuers*. Washington, DC: SEC.

SEC. 2007b. *Release No. 8879, Acceptance from Foreign Private Issuers of Financial Statements Prepared in Accordance with IFRS without Reconciliation to U.S. GAAP*. Washington, DC: SEC.

SEC. October, 2009. Strategic Plan For Fiscal Years 2010—2015—Draft Smith, L. M. for Comments, www.sec.gov/about/secstratplan1015.pdf

SEC. 2011. *SEC Charges Military Body Armor Supplier and Former Outside Directors with Accounting Fraud*. Washington, DC: SEC.

SEC. 2014. Form 10-K. http://www.sec.gov/answers/form10k.htm

SEC. 2016. Montana, https://www.sec.gov/news/pressrelease/2016-25.html

Sharma, S., M. Joshi, and M. Kansal. 2017. "IFRS adoption challenges in developing economies: an Indian perspective." *Managerial Auditing Journal*. 32, no. 4/5. pp. 406–426.

Standard and Poor. February, 2004. Monthly Report: World by Numbers. www.standardandpoors.com/spf/pdf/index/worldbynumbers_Jan04.pdf

Standard and Poor. September, 2009. Monthly Report: World by Numbers. www.standardandpoors.com/spf/pdf/index/WBN_Sept09.pdf

Street, D.L. 2002. "Benchmarking National Accounting Standards against IAS: Summary of Results." *Journal of International Accounting, Auditing and Taxation* 11, no. 1, pp. 77–94.

Street, D.L. 2011. *Criteria for an Independent Accounting Standard Setter. How Does the IASB Rate?* Washington, D.C.: Council of Institutional Investors.

Street, D., S. Gray, and S. Bryant. 1999. "Acceptance and Observance of International Accounting Standards: An Empirical Study of Companies Claiming to Comply with IASs." *International Journal of Accounting* 34, no. 1, pp. 11–48.

Swanton, M. June, 2007. "GCs Under Fire." *Inside Counsel* 17, no. 187, p. 13.

Tsunogaya, N., A. Hellman, S.D. Scagnelli. 2015. "Adoption of IFRS in Japan." *Pacific Accounting Review* 27, no. 1, pp. 3–27.

Tsunogaya, N. 2016. "Issues Affecting Decisions on Mandatory Adoption of International Financial Reporting Standards (IFRS) in Japan." *Accounting, Auditing and Accountability Journal,* 29, no. 5 pp. 828–860.

Uzma, S.H. 2016. "Cost-benefit Analysis of IFRS Adoption: Developed and Emerging Countries." *Journal of Financial Reporting and Accounting* 14, no. 2, pp. 198–229.

Walker, R.G. 1987. "Australia's ARSB: A Case Study of Political Activity and Regulatory Capture." *Accounting and Business Research* 17, no. 67, pp. 269–286.

White, M.J.A. 2017. A U.S. Imperative: High Quality, Globally Accepted Accounting Standards. https://www.sec.gov/news/statement/white-2016-01-05.html

Yallapragada, R.R. March, 2012. "Incorporating International Financial Reporting Standards into the United States Financial Reporting System: Timeline and Implications." *International Business and Economics Research Journal* 11, no. 3, pp. 283–290.

Zeff, S. 2013. "The Objectives of Financial Reporting: A Historical Survey and Analysis." *Accounting and Business Research* 43, no. 4, pp. 262–327.

Zeff, S. and C. Nobes. 2010. "Commentary: Has Australia (or Any Other Jurisdiction) 'Adopted' IFRS?" *Australian Accounting Review* 20, no. 2, pp. 178–184.

# About the Authors

**Roger Hussey** is a member of the Association of Chartered Certified Accountants and holds an MSc and a PhD from Bath University, United Kingdom. Following a 6-year research position at the Oxford University, he accepted the post of Deloitte Professor at the University of the West of England. In 2000, he became dean of the Odette School of Business at the University of Windsor, Canada. He is emeritus professor at both the University of the West of England and the University of Windsor, Canada.

**Audra Ong** received her PhD from the University of the West of England, MBA from the University of Wales, Cardiff, and BSc in accounting from Queen's University of Belfast, United Kingdom. She has published in academic journals and is coauthor of *Strategic Cost Analysis*, published by Business Expert Press. She taught in the United Kingdom before moving to University of Windsor, where she is professor of accounting.

# Index

# OTHER TITLES IN OUR FINANCIAL ACCOUNTING AND AUDITING COLLECTION

Mark Bettner, Bucknell University and
Michael Coyne, Fairfield University, *Editors*

- *Accounting for Fun and Profit: A Guide to Understanding Advanced Topics in Accounting* by Lawrence A. Weiss
- *Accounting History and the Rise of Civilization, Volume I* by Gary Giroux
- *Accounting History and the Rise of Civilization, Volume II* by Gary Giroux
- *A Refresher in Financial Accounting* by Faisal Sheikh
- *Accounting Fraud, Second Edition: Maneuvering and Manipulation, Past and Present* by Gary Giroux
- *Corporate Governance in the Aftermath of the Global Financial Crisis, Volume I: Relevance and Reforms* by Zabihollah Rezaee
- *Corporate Governance in the Aftermath of the Global Financial Crisis, Volume II: Functions and Sustainability* by Zabihollah Rezaee
- *Corporate Governance in the Aftermath of the Global Financial Crisis, Volume III: Gatekeeper Functions* by Zabihollah Rezaee
- *Corporate Governance in the Aftermath of the Global Financial Crisis, Volume IV: Emerging Issues in Corporate Governance* by Zabihollah Rezaee
- *Using Accounting & Financial Information, Second Edition: Analyzing, Forecasting, and Decision Making* by Mark S. Bettner

CPSIA information can be obtained
at www.ICGtesting.com
Printed in the USA
LVHW081517110521
687107LV00014B/609